ERDMUTH JO[...]
and Lucia Gro[...]
He studied eurythmy and education at the Goetheanum in Dornach, Switzerland. After working as a eurythmist for a number of years on the Goetheanum stage, he taught eurythmy in Waldorf schools in Germany and Denmark, and later worked as class teacher and upper school history, art history and eurythmy teacher in the Rudolf Steiner School in Basel. He then studied industrial psychology at the Institute for Applied Psychology in Zurich, where he later worked. He was involved in various training programmes for leaders in industry and commerce, as well as in state institutions. Grosse then worked freelance as a management consultant and as a lecturer in anthroposophy in Switzerland, Germany and Denmark. He died in 2012.

ARE THERE PEOPLE WITHOUT A SELF?

On the Mystery of the Ego and the
Appearance in the Present Day
of Egoless Individuals

Erdmuth Johannes Grosse

Translated by Paul King

TEMPLE LODGE

With heartfelt thanks to my dear wife, Renate Grosse-Meuter, for her great interest in the writing of this book; it gave rise to many good ideas.

Temple Lodge Publishing Ltd.
Hillside House, The Square
Forest Row, RH18 5ES

www.templelodge.com

Published in English by Temple Lodge in 2021

Originally published in German under the title *Gibt es Menschen ohne ein Ich?: Über die Mysterien des Ich und das Erscheinen ichloser Menschen in der Gegenwart* by Verlag für Anthroposophie, Dornach, Switzerland, in 2018. This translation is based on the fourth edition, 2019

© Verlag für Anthroposophie, Dornach 2018
This translation © Temple Lodge Publishing 2021

A CIP catalogue record for this book is available from the British Library

ISBN 978 1 912230 80 8

Cover by Morgan Creative
Typeset by Symbiosys Technologies, Visakhapatnam, India
Printed and bound by 4Edge Ltd., Essex

Contents

'...that in our times a kind of supernumerary person is appearing who is egoless, who in reality is not a human being. This is a terrible truth.'

Rudolf Steiner [1]

Translator's note on use of the term 'Ego'

The German word *Ich* is translated in this book interchangeably as Ego (with capital E) or I. In this context Ego does not refer to what we could call the 'lower ego', to our selfish nature of petty conceits and self-centredness. Rather, it refers to our 'higher Ego', to the I-am core of our being which aspires to become a more understanding, more empathetic, more conscientious and nobler human being. Most essentially in the framework of the book, the Ego is that aspect of our being which incarnates from life to life on earth.

Translator's interpolations in the text are indicated by curly brackets {like this}.

Paul King

Foreword

This book is about people who do not have a human Ego. The significance of this was spoken about by Rudolf Steiner in lectures, meetings and conversations. Egoless individuals are empty sheaths through which other beings can operate.

The phenomenon of egolessness is not something that affects only the destiny of the egoless individual; this deficiency in egoless people represents a problem with possible negative consequences for all humanity.

Egoless individuals can be businesspeople, ministers, opinion-makers, leaders of sects, and members of political parties. Their influence in our present civilization is particularly active through occult Lodges that prefer to remain in the background from where they direct the careers of young politicians.

In working on this theme it occurred to me to try to give it a 'musical' composition. This arises of itself when, for example, we contrast the subject of *egolessness* with *Johan Gottlieb Fichte*. We see this when we look at characteristic situations in Fichte's life which exhibit a particularly strong Ego-force.

The first quarter of the book looks at the esoteric aspect of the Ego. What is meant by this is that we only know a limited part of ourselves—the exoteric part. We need to take on the laborious work of discovering the hidden part.

We hear the exhortation of the Guardian: 'O Man, know thyself!' That we do not yet know ourselves is something necessary for our development, for only by effort do we develop the inner forces that take us forward.

The themes result in a garland of ideas which, when we think them through, have a contrapuntal quality.

I am aware that this subject is a delicate one and could lead
to many misunderstandings. I would therefore like to state here
expressly that the content of this book is not intended at any
point or in any way to discriminate against or discredit anyone.

Ermuth Johannes Grosse
Dornach, Autumn 2011

Introduction: The Ego
and its sheaths

This book takes the reader into the riddle of the human Ego. At the same time it is an introduction to Rudolf Steiner's anthroposophy which is the foundation upon which this work is based.

Through his clairvoyant research and the way in which Rudolf Steiner was able to present the results of this research and make them comprehensible, we are encouraged to take up the supersensory element into our thoughts and thus leave the physical and material realm.

Our principal subjects are the Ego and the spiritual evolution of the human being. By thinking along the lines of Steiner's work, the reader, who becomes a spiritual student, enters on the path of self-schooling. In this context they can come up against the problem of the existence of people who do not have an Ego—or more precisely, a *human* Ego—whereby impulses that obstruct development can enter into humanity as a whole.

The book leads on to some of the fundamental ideas of anthroposophy which are dealt with briefly: the Ego 'lives' in envelopes or sheaths through which it can act in the world. Rudolf Steiner calls these 'members-of-being,' which the spiritual researcher can perceive spiritually.

What does a researcher of the spirit see?

> When we are awake during the day there is in our human being what we call the four members of human nature—physical body, etheric body, astral body, and Ego—connected together, we could say, in a certain regulated way. We can best show the proper connection between these four members of human nature if we draw it in the way that clairvoyant consciousness sees the so-called human aura. What I can draw for you is naturally only very sketchy.
>
> So if we look at the usual waking condition of the human being, we would draw the auric make-up of the person in roughly

the following way [see Illustration 1]: the physical body with the
darker line; the etheric body inside the dotted line; the line with
larger shadings is the astral body; and the Ego aura would be
drawn permeating the whole human being. But I'll draw it as rays
which, without any limits, surround the individual upwards and
downwards like rays.

Next to this I'll draw the difference in the auric make-up of
a person who is asleep, at around midnight, or rather the auric
picture of the person [see illustration 2]: physical body and etheric
body are as in the first drawing; the darker shaded lines represent
the astral body, it continues downwards indefinitely and rises out
{of the body}, but it remains in a vertical position. I would then
have to draw the Ego aura in the form of rays, as we see here.

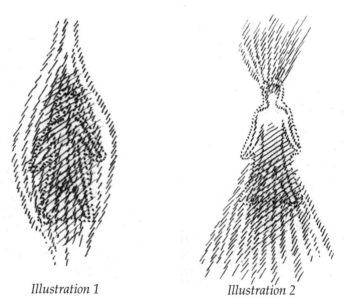

Illustration 1   *Illustration 2*

The Ego aura is interrupted in the region of the throat and only
recommences in the region of the head, but raying outwards, and
goes upwards where it becomes indistinct—the person is in a
horizontal position, but it is directed upwards from the head. So,
essentially, the appearance of the aura of a sleeping person is such

that the astral body is substantially condensed and dark—the shaded area in the drawing—but in its upper parts is thinner than during the day. The Ego aura is interrupted in the throat region, it is radial again below and extends until it becomes indistinct.

The important point is that, in the sleeping state, what we can call the auric image of the Ego is in fact split into two parts. Whereas in the waking condition the Ego aura coheres in an oval form, during sleep it divides in the middle and consists of two parts; one of these is turned downwards by a kind of weight, and spreads out downwards, so that we do not find an enclosed Ego aura but one that extends downwards. For clairvoyant consciousness this part of the Ego aura appears as an essentially darker part of the aura that has dark strands that are nuanced, for example, with strong tinges of darkish red. The part that separates upwards is again such that it runs narrowly from the head region, then spreads out and becomes indistinct, expands so to speak, into the world of stars. The astral body is not separated in the middle in the same way, so we can't speak of an actual separation of the astral body, whereas the Ego aura, at least for our vision, is split.

So in this occult view we also have a pictorial expression of the fact that the human being {during sleep} goes, with the Ego forces that permeate him during his waking state, out into cosmic spaces in order to connect with the starry world, to imbibe, as it were, the forces of the world of stars.

Now the part of the Ego aura that separates off downwards and becomes dark, appears more or less opaque (whereas the part going upwards glows and shines brightly, radiates in bright light), and is the part most exposed to the ahrimanic powers. The part of the astral body bordering it is the most exposed to the luciferic forces. So we can say: the property we justifiably attribute to the Ego and astral body, {namely} that they leave the human being, is absolutely accurate for the *upper portions* of the Ego and astral aura. It is not applicable for the parts of the Ego and astral aura that correspond more to the lower portions, particularly the lower portions of the human trunk: for these parts it is even the case that during sleep the auras of the Ego and astral body are *more* inside, more bound up with the physical and etheric bodies than they are in the waking state, that going down they are denser and more compact. For we also see that, in the process of waking up, what I have drawn so strongly down below departs again from the lower parts of our being. Just as the upper part departs as we fall asleep, so the lower part of the Ego and astral aura departs in a certain way when we wake up, and only a kind of portion of these two auras remains inside, as I have shown in the first figure.

Now it is of equal and exceptional importance to know that, through the evolution of our earth, through all the forces that have played their part in this, and which you can find in {my book} *Occult Science*,[2] things are arranged so that the human being does not participate in this energetic work of the lower aura during sleep, or rather does not participate as a witness. For it is in these parts of the lower Ego aura and the lower astral aura that the enlivening forces are stimulated which are needed by human beings in order to restore what is used up during the waking state. The restorative forces have to emerge from these parts of the aura. The fact that they work upwards and restore the whole human being depends on the development of forces of attraction in the portion of aura that departs upwards, which it imbibes from the world of stars. With these forces it {the upper aura} is able to attract the forces coming from below so that they have a regenerative effect on the human being. This is the objective process.[3]

Rudolf Steiner here clarifies the interaction between the four members-of-being: physical body, etheric body, astral body, and Ego.

If we try to think along the lines of these processes and gain an idea of them in our minds, we take the first steps on the path of an esoteric development. In doing so we release the etheric body in our head region from being shackled to the physical body, whereby the etheric body begins to flow more strongly and to form the basis of a thinking that is not exclusively bound to the physical brain.

Are there people without an Ego?

The question as to whether there is such a thing as individuals who do not have an Ego, leads us initially to another question— the question namely as to what kind of being the human being is.

This question is answered comprehensively by Rudolf Steiner's anthroposophy. Taking this answer and focusing on what is presented in it as the question of the Ego, we can say: the human is a being that has an Ego {or 'I'} as its spiritual centre.

What is an Ego?

In his book *Theosophy*,[4] Rudolf Steiner quotes from the autobiography of the poet Jean Paul (1763-1825) who relates the following:

> I shall never forget the event I have told no-one about, when I found myself at the birth of my self-consciousness, for which I can give the exact time and place. As a very young child I was standing one morning at the door of the house and looking to my left at the woodpile, when all at once the inner perception hit me like a bolt of lightning: 'I am an I', and ever since has remained glowingly with me. That was the first time and for all eternity that my I saw itself. Illusions of memory are hard to imagine here, since no alien story could mix additions into an occurrence taking place purely in the veiled holy of holies of the human being, and whose novelty is given an enduring quality just because of the everyday circumstances.

Rudolf Steiner finishes Jean Paul's anecdote and continues:

> It is well known that little children refer to themselves by saying, 'Carl is good,' 'Mary wants...' We find it natural that they talk about themselves as though of another person, because they are not yet conscious of their independent being, because the awareness of self is not yet born in them. Through self-awareness the human being regards himself as an independent being, a being enclosed from everything else, an 'I'.

> In the 'I' {or Ego} the human being summarizes everything he
> experiences as a corporeal, mental and emotional being. Body
> and soul are the bearers of the 'I'; it operates in them.[5]

The Ego is thus the human individual as a spiritual being. It travels along the path of its individual development through many earth lives. In each life on earth, in an alternation of karma from within and karma from without, it undergoes its biography which gives shape and expression to its very own unique life-motif.

Development always consists of developmental impulses. From where does the Ego draw its developmental impulses? The answer is: it draws them from itself. This is to be understood in the sense that the Ego requires two gestures for its development. On the one hand it must open itself in order to receive new spiritual impulses; on the other hand it develops by overcoming obstacles that approach it both from outside and from within, from its own being. This gives rise to strength of Ego which shows itself as sound judgement, resilience, and purposefulness. So it is both a humble gesture of self-opening towards higher powers, and a courageous stance in face of the challenges of life through which our inner being is consolidated.

Deeply rooted in the nature of the Ego is the will to evolve: I will progress, I will discard the qualities in myself that impede me, so that my true being can unfold.

That this will to evolve can be hidden by minor matters in the hustle-and-bustle of everyday life or by negative (unfavourable) relationships, is something that initially we simply have to accept. But its voice is raised in the high moments of life. Whether this voice is heard in the ongoing hubbub of daily entanglements depends on whether a person is a spirit-seeker or just lets themself be driven along passively.

Fundamentally the human being does not know who he is. What is meant by this is that it is difficult for him to fathom the spiritual depths of his Ego.

This thought leads us to look in a more differentiated way at the Ego. When we observe little children we see that they bump themselves, that they have many—often painful—collisions. But these are necessary because the child becomes aware of itself through the bumps. Ego-consciousness arises through collisions.

> The child gets to know itself through the external world, and in the first years the whole of life actually consists of the child learning to discriminate itself from the external world and to know itself by means of the external world. And the result of a sufficient number of collisions with the outer world is summarized in the child's soul as its awareness of itself.[6]

What we experience as our Ego in waking life is our *ego-consciousness*, which is interrupted every time we sleep; it is the exoteric side of our Ego. The esoteric side of our Ego wants to elude our conscious soul-spiritual apprehension. It is the actual core of our being, which passes through many lives on earth, experiencing and shaping its karma.

At the age of 20, Friedrich Nietzsche wrote a poem entitled 'To the Unknown God'. He describes in it a search for himself, for his own deeper being, for the esoteric side of his Ego. There he experiences the 'unknown god'.

To the Unknown God[7]

Once more, before I move onward
and turn my gaze ahead,
in loneliness I lift my hands to you,
you to whom I flee,
to whom I, in the deepest depths of my heart,
solemnly consecrated altars
so that ever
your voice may call to me again.

Deeply engraved in those altars
glows the phrase: To The Unknown God.

> I am his, although I have, even up to this hour,
> also stayed among the sacrilegious horde;
> I am his—and I feel the snares
> that pull me down in the struggle and,
> though I might flee,
> compel me nevertheless into his service.
> I want to know you, O Unknown One,
> Who reaches deep into my soul,
> Who roams through my life like a storm—
> You Unfathomable One, akin to me!
> I want to know you, even serve you.

The unknown side of our being, of our Ego, that is hidden from us, is the unknown god. That this is ultimately the Christ—as preached by St Paul in his Areopagus sermon at Athens—is the very core and deepest aspect of the Ego mysteries, and Nietzsche has an intimation of this in his poem. It deals with the fact that, in our Ego, we can open ourselves to Christ and thus overcome a hardening in the Ego and lack of progress in spiritual development.

We may feel it to be a shortcoming on our part that our actual being is hidden from us in daily life. Why may we not know at every moment of our lives who we really are? Concerning this, Rudolf Steiner says the following:

> We might perhaps raise a complaint against the gods, if I may use this expression, that they have put the most valuable aspect for the human being in the hidden side of his life, that they have not made manifest, as it were, what is of greatest value in him. Had they done so, the human being would in a higher sense remain powerless. We gain soul-spiritual forces that can then permeate our whole existence, precisely because we first have to achieve our actual human value and being, because we have first to *do* something at the soul and spiritual level, in order to become a human being at all in the proper sense. And it is in this overcoming, in this necessity of first doing something in order to become a human being, that there lies what makes us strong, what can permeate us with forces precisely in the innermost of our being.[8]

This section of the lecture points us to the fact that, in the course of our development, we must first seek our true being. Whether consciously or not, every human being is a *Seeker of Oneself* (as in the title of the novel by Albert Steffen). It is the *higher Ego*[9] that the human being is seeking. It is what is realized in spirit-self, step by step in every life, and what we strive towards in collaboration with our angel. The higher Ego is living, so to speak, in the plan of this development, and asserts itself as the will to evolve.

With our Ego we pass through many lives. We experience and shape our destiny and, through our own intention, are constantly adding new karmic situations to the old. The new here is a creative element that is born out of the depths of our being, often through pain and difficulties. All positivity, open-mindedness, and forgiveness are a part of this. And also our aesthetic and intellectual judgement. Rudolf Steiner calls this new element created by human beings out of their freedom, 'creation out of nothing'. This is born out of the power of the Ego. It lies beyond what is required of us by karma. It is a free deed, a free addition to the course of the world. The archai— the time-spirits which the spiritual researcher also calls Spirits of Personality—find 'nourishment' in these creations out of nothing. Steiner presents this interaction between humanity and the hierarchy of archai in the lecture cycle *Geisteswissen-schaftliche Menschenkunde*[10] (Spiritual-scientific knowledge of the human being), as follows:

> What people create from epoch to epoch, from age to age, as the results of logical thinking, of aesthetic sensibility, of fulfilment of their duties, forms an on-flowing tide, it provides matter and substance into which the Spirits of Personality embed themselves in their present development.
>
> This is how you live your life, this is how you develop further. And while you develop, the Spirits of Personality gaze down on you and constantly ask, 'Are you also giving me something I can use for my own development?' And the more we develop

the content of our thinking, our wealth of thought, the more we try to refine our aesthetic feeling, to fulfil our duty over and above what karma requires, the more nourishment the Spirits of Personality have; the more we offer up to them, the more these Spirits of Personality become denser in their bodily nature. [...] But what humankind puts into the supersensory realm through its development, is food and drink for these Spirits of Personality; they relish it. If there were a time in which people lived without developing a richness of thought, without pleasure or displeasure [ohne Gefallen oder Missfallen], without a sense of duty that went beyond the mere drives of karma—in such a time the Spirits of Personality would have nothing to eat, they would become thin. In this way our life is connected to invisible beings who suffuse and permeate our life.[11]

This brief description of the results of spiritual research can put us in optimistic mood. We are not subjected to an evolution that simply steamrolls over us as it advances blindly onward, but we can contribute to the course of the world something of our own that is rooted in the core of our being and can counterpose the forces of decline with upward-striving human forces of the Ego.

In the *creation out of nothing* we have a spiritual fact that shows in the strongest way what it means to possess an Ego and to act out of it.

We can summarize the nature of the Ego: It can open itself to a higher principle and receive spiritual impulses. In doing so it becomes inwardly enriched. And it can consolidate its forces by overcoming obstacles.

The image of the caduceus {or staff of Mercury} is an impressive symbol of the nature of the Ego—one of many possible symbols. The two serpents entwining symmetrically around the straight vertical staff, show the Ego's to-and-fro oscillation between the luciferic and the ahrimanic principles. In the caduceus symbol this movement is harmoniously balanced so that the luciferic and ahrimanic principles neutralize each other.

Everyone who looks at their own development is aware that this state of balance is an ideal condition seldom achieved. Yet the caduceus represents the kingly power of the Ego behind the spiritual striving of each individual, and by which again and again the individual finds their centre.

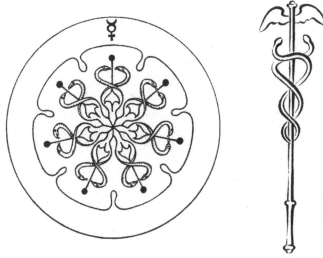

The Caduceus (drawing), fifth
planetary seal by
Rudolf Steiner

The Caduceus
{Staff of Mercury}, a symbol of
the nature of the Ego

Dementia and the Ego

Before we address this subject we need to discuss the phenomenon of dementia itself. The Ego can only operate when it possesses a functional physical body as its 'instrument'. This instrument includes the brain. If we refer to a person with dementia as 'feeble-minded' or 'stupid', we do them an injustice. Their Ego can be highly spiritual, but this spirituality cannot come to expression because of the unsuitability of the instrument. Their mental forces are blocked in this life only to unfold with perhaps powerful energy in the next incarnation.

In his *Curative Education* course[12] Rudolf Steiner discussed children in need of special care. I well remember one of these children, a boy called Sandroe Stoughton, an American who lived with us because my father, Rudolf Grosse, was looking after him. In Lecture 6 Steiner says of him: 'You may believe me or not, but this boy is a genius.'[13] Due to his karmic circumstances however, he could only find a physical body that his Ego and astral body could not take proper hold of. 'They bump up against something rock-like in the organism.'

Sandroe was a special person who despite his handicap had something very spiritual about him. Later on, when he was no longer living with us, he would sometimes come to visit, and then I could experience this quality in him. He loved the great classical dramas of German literature, with which he had a non-intellectual connection, particularly the *Maid of Orleans* by Schiller and Goethe's *Faust*, and Rudolf Steiner's *Mystery Dramas* which were performed at the Goetheanum in Dornach.

Are there people who don't have an Ego? On the basis of Rudolf Steiner's research the answer to this question must be yes. However, for a definition of egolessness we must first consider some basic points to give us a perspective of the full range of the question. We can picture egolessness as a phenomenon that appears in varying degrees of intensity, ranging from a weak Ego to the complete absence of a human Ego.

But we need to note that egolessness means the absence of a *human* Ego. The vacant space is occupied by other beings— elemental beings, nature demons, ahrimanic or luciferic beings— so that a person of this nature can have a strong influence, albeit a non-human one.

Ego weakness can be observed in multiple ways in everyday life. It shows itself in being easily influenced, in lack of discern- ment, in the inability to make decisions—in short, a picture that applies to the majority of humankind, to 'the masses'. Each of us can also find situations like this in our own lives and in our own existence as an Ego. We realize they can arise from time to time and depend on the state of our bodily nature or, more precisely, on the harmonious or disharmonious interaction of body, soul, and spirit. In these cases Ego weakness can be effectively treated using a medical, pedagogical or psychological approach. The sit- uation here is not a matter of absence of Ego but, as stated above, of insufficient penetration by the Ego.

Demonic beings

We can now also imagine an Ego weakness that is not healed from within but is stabilized from the outside. This gives rise to a façade of Ego solidity. Here, however, it is not the actual Ego of the affected person who has found their own strength, but an immovable rigidity of Ego arises which can have great energy and vigour but is inhuman. What is meant here can be observed in our present-day business world in the typical picture of the cold manager (e.g. the investment bank Lehman Brothers). It comes about by being impregnated by an ideology or by a fixation on a material goal. Here too we must distinguish many possible gradations. But a person of this nature does not act out of themselves but is more or less strongly possessed. This means that their weak Ego is ousted by another being.

What follows is a particularly gripping example of a situation where the Ego leaves its sheaths and a foreign being enters and occupies them.

In his autobiography *Blick durchs Prisma, Lebensbericht eines Arztes*[14] (Looking through a Prism: Account of a doctor's life), the anthroposophical doctor Wilhelm zur Linden (1896-1972), who for some decades had a practice in Berlin, describes this case:

> The incident I am about to describe is one of the most harrowing experiences I ever encountered as a doctor. Even today I have not got over it. On the rare occasions when I have related it to a small group of people there have frequently been those who had some kind of ready-made standard explanation for it; I myself know, however, that such explanations give us no real understanding. Only someone who has never experienced anything like this would be satisfied with such a 'diagnosis'.
>
> I am including the incident here because the events, which took place more than twenty-one years ago, were reawakened in me a few months ago when I happened to meet once more one of

the people involved. This gave me the opportunity to check and test the accuracy of my memory, for, at my prompting, the lady in question could remember many details and was able to confirm the clarity of my recall even of minor details.

During the early years of the war, my revered colleague, Dr Paul Jaerschky, one of the early campaigners for natural medical treatment in Germany, asked me to take on the further treatment of one of his most severe cases. He was ill himself and impeded by advanced old age.

The patient was a military officer with the rank of general, whose name I will naturally not mention. He was suffering from a metastasised cancer of the sacrum which was treated with radiation and large doses of Iscador. The man, who was nearly two metres tall, had been lying for nine months on his stomach and was virtually immobilized by the extraordinary pain of the illness. He was an exceptionally refined, introverted person, from whom I heard hardly a word of complaint. He clearly had the very best relationship with his wife, who was also a person of great refinement. I cannot remember whether the couple had any connection with anthroposophy or the Christian Community, but they were definitely religious.

There were three children: the eldest, aged 35, was a graduate engineer; the second, somewhat younger, was also an engineer; and a daughter, aged 28, who at that time was a nurse working in a military hospital.

The sickbed that Herr W had to endure was harrowing. I tried as far as was possible to assuage his afflictions. One could only wish for him that he die soon, but his time had clearly not yet come. Over the course of weeks a connection developed between us based, for my part, on the greatest regard for his valiant inner attitude, and his refined humanity. Due to the great demands on me in my duties as a military doctor and in my civilian practice, I was only able to find time to visit every few days.

One day, Frau W. rang and asked me to come quickly and to bring my old doctor friend Dr Jaerschky, because her husband

had said he was now dying, and expressed the wish to say good-
bye to his two doctors.

It was not until late evening that I had time to cross half of
Berlin, and picked up my colleague Jaerschky, who had been sick
in bed.

When we entered the flat we were astonished to find our
patient lying on his back for the first time in months. In the morning he had told his family that, as an old soldier, he did not want
the undertakers to find him lying on his stomach. He had told his
children to take hold of him, each one on a leg or arm, and then
gave the command to turn him over. How he managed to bear
this without the strongest doses of painkillers was an enigma to
us doctors. He had then called his children to him one by one,
told each one their weaknesses and their good qualities, and gave
them advice on how to conduct themselves in the future.

His sons, whom one could certainly not describe as tending
towards sentimentality, were most strongly moved and impressed
by the goodness and wisdom of their father.

Towards evening he became weaker and weaker, and when
we doctors arrived at his bedside at around eleven o'clock, he had
hardly any discernible pulse and had great difficulty speaking.
Dr Jaerschky bent close to his ear, spoke to him and prayed with
him. The collapse of his forces advanced quickly, and shortly
before midnight he was on the point of dying. Dr Jaerschky suddenly became very weak and asked me to take him home, which
I did as my clear duty. The dying man was barely aware of our
departure; our leave-taking was calm and ceremonial.

Around four in the morning, Frau W. rang once more: 'Doctor, please come immediately. Something terrible has happened.'
Although I could hear from her tone of voice that something very
unusual must have occurred, in my over-tiredness I said, 'But,
dear lady, he could only have died. What else could it be?' She
answered, 'No, it's something quite dreadful. Please come.'

When I entered the bedroom a good hour later I found Herr W.
lying on his front again, but with his head at the foot of the bed.

Supporting himself on his arms he lifted himself up and bellowed at me with a loud voice, and looked at me with the eyes of a wild animal. Apoplectic with rage, barking out orders in the harshest tone of voice, he made all sorts of demands for food and whatever. All that remained of his previous refinement, politeness and modesty, and even of his facial expression and way of speaking, was a travesty, a wild distortion. He seethed in wild frenzy and spat out swearwords that even I, as a soldier on the front for many years, had never heard. That he was capable of lifting his upper body at all was completely incomprehensible to me.

A completely different being, like a ravening demon, was speaking out of the body of the humanly so refined and endearing Herr W. A cancer patient who for months had been approaching his end, and who used his last reserves of strength to say farewell to his family and doctors, until he succumbed to the throes of death—how could he shortly afterwards fall into such a frenzy? The transformation was as terrible as it was medically incomprehensible.

I can no longer remember when—that is, how soon after our departure—this gruesome change had began. He had certainly not received an injection of a stimulant or the like. We left the house at around half past twelve, and Frau W. rang me for help at around four, after delaying to do so for as long as she could out of consideration for me.

We came to the conclusion that we could not be dealing with the 'deceased' who was so dear to us, but that at the moment of death his body had been possessed by a demon. All attempts by clever people to 'explain' this experience are of no help, they are completely inadequate. I have considered them myself, but there is no point in listing them here.

I tried to somehow calm the 'beast'. But after three days Frau W. had got to the point where—unheard by the others—she said to me, 'If only the brute would get on with it and die!' This was a very egregious thing to come out of the mouth of this refined and loving lady. But it shows perhaps most clearly what the situation really was. It was simply unbearable to have to deal with this being any longer.

I was particularly busy during that period and could only rarely find time to visit the W. household. This ghastly situation went on for nearly a fortnight before the possessed body was finally left in peace.

In the time following this I often thought the whole thing had been just a horrible dream. The events of the war pushed everything else aside; because of my views I had to deal with some serious chicaneries by some of my colleagues which resulted in my being sent to the front. I finally landed up in Prague.

Around two years later I was working as head doctor in the kidney hospital in Radlice, Prague. One day while I was doing my rounds I was addressed by a very tall sergeant who seemed to know me. It turned out he was the eldest son of General W. When there were just the two of us he said, 'Doctor, do you still remember the terrible story of my father's death?' My doubts about the reality of those events were now finally laid to rest. We talked through the whole affair once more. And then, nearly twenty-two years later in the spring of 1963, I saw the daughter, who gave me the second confirmation.

But can a doctor in our times really venture to talk seriously about a person being possessed by a demon!? I believe the answer is yes. However, it certainly requires intellectual courage. I am even convinced of the necessity for all of us to learn to pay heed once more to the devastating effect of demonic beings in the world.

The sages of past times knew a great deal about demons, even if we leave aside Christ and the Bible. Are we still going to regard our forefathers, from whom we are descended after all, as limited and stupid? Their way of thinking was certainly different from our own, but was it any less related to reality? The existence of demons was certain knowledge for them. Incidentally, this question has recently come under serious discussion from another direction.

This is not the right place for a detailed discussion on the origin and incidence of 'demonic beings'. I consider we should stop imagining evil in such an abstract, anonymous and non-committal way as is usually done despite the prevalence of actual experiences, but rather as concretely and 'in-the-flesh' as possible. Even Luther threw his inkwell at the devil, Goethe spoke of demonic beings with regard to Napoleon, and modern authors like, for example, Gustav Würtenberg also speak of them. Würtenberg gave his 1947 book the title *Nero oder die Macht der Dämonen* (Nero or the power of demons), by which he actually meant Hitler. I know many individuals of Hitler's immediate entourage, and am inclined to attribute the sudden radical changes in his nature which transformed him from a colourless, almost tiresome philistine into a raging creature of downright inhuman proportion, to possession by demons.

Wilhem zur Linden is here describing his encounter with a demon who takes hold of the sheaths of a dying man. With its cursing it disturbs the mood of solemnity that arises when a person comes to the end of their life on earth and crosses the threshold to the spiritual world.

What is a demon?

A demon is a spiritual being that is active within the sphere of evil. Being itself evil, it tries to tempt human beings into doing evil.

The first step into this consists in creating a mood in which what is spiritually elevated is made to look ridiculous, and what is vile is made to appear in keeping with human nature.

Goethe writes a conversation between Faust and Mephistopheles about the task of evil:

> Faust: 'Very well, so who are you?'
> Mephistopheles: '...{I am} a part of the force that always seeks to do evil and always creates good.'[15]

Why is this so? Because, in his encounters with evil, the human being strengthens his forces which he can then employ to overcome and transform evil.

A particular characteristic of the events related by Wilhelm zur Linden should be noted: the people involved experienced the demon with their physical senses.

They heard it swearing. It had entered the physical world. As a rule, however, demons penetrate into the human astral aura and exert an influence at a subconscious level.

What is the nature of the Ego?

Before we continue, let us ask: What is the Ego, and how can we understand its nature?

We can find an answer to this in the figure of Faust as created by Goethe and as painted by Rudolf Steiner in the cupola painting of the first Goetheanum.

This figure of Faust expresses the human Ego.

Faust, the representative of the seeking human being striving for knowledge, who appears in the dome of the smaller cupola out of the mysterious, mystical blue, is striving towards the fully conscious 'I', the I that expresses itself in the word.

The word *Ich* {i.e. the German word for *I*} is shaped and painted in such a way that the viewer experiences this written word as forming a unity with Faust's gesture; Faust—the one who thinks from his Ego-strength, who experiences his I—is given form by the artist Rudolf Steiner out of the flooding colour of the small cupola of the first Goetheanum as a human being bearing an Ego [*Ich-Mensch*]. In this work of art the viewer grasps the Ego intuitively, not intellectually.

What task does the Ego have throughout the individual's incarnations on earth? It has the task of developing an individual relationship to the Mystery of Golgotha, to Christ, whose initials, **Jesus Christ**, constitute the word 'Ich'.

The Ego of another person cannot be directly perceived clairvoyantly by a spiritual researcher, unlike the self-teaching impulses that arise from the Ego. These are evident in a person's aura as an organizing, spiritualizing force. 'The workings of the Ego in the aura can be seen by a seer. The Ego itself is invisible even to him. It is truly the "veiled holy of holies" in the human being.'[16]

Faust, the seeker of knowledge, strives to develop a fully conscious Ego. (Painting of the small cupola of the first Goetheanum, the Faust motif.)

The sense of Ego

The Ego can however be grasped by a non-clairoyant process of observation. How? By the *sense of Ego*. We have twelve senses, of which the sense of Ego is the most spiritual. With this sense we perceive the Ego of another person.

This act of perception is a complex process which Rudolf Steiner describes in a course of lectures, *Allegemine Menschenkunde als Grundlage der Pädagogik*[17] (Study of Man), given to the teachers of the Waldorf School, as follows:

> It is something different when I perceive my own Ego in my interior than when I recognize another person as an Ego. The perception of another's Ego depends on the sense of Ego just as the perception of colour depends on the sense of sight, and sound on the sense of hearing. [...] The organ of perception of other Egos is dispersed over the whole human being and consists of a very subtle substantiality, which is why people do not speak about an organ for the sense of Ego. This organ for the sense of Ego is something different from what brings about my experience of my own Ego. [...] For, perceiving the Ego of another person is essentially a cognitive process, or at least similar to one; experiencing one's own Ego by contrast is a will process. [...]
>
> When you have someone before you, what happens is the following: You perceive the person for a brief time; they make an impression on you. This impression causes a disturbance in your interior: you feel that the person, who is actually the same kind of being as yourself, is making an impression on you like an attack. The consequence is that you inwardly defend yourself, that you resist this attack, that you become inwardly aggressive towards it. You then start to flag in this aggression, the aggression ceases, and the other person can then make an impression on you once more. This gives you time to increase your aggressive energy again, and you carry out another piece of aggression. You flag again, and the

> other person again makes an impression on you, and so on. This
> is the relation that exists when one person stands before another
> one perceiving their Ego: openness to the person—inner defence;
> openness to the other—inner defence; sympathy—antipathy; sym-
> pathy—antipathy. What I am talking about here is not about our
> feeling life but purely about perceiving something in front of us.
> The soul vibrates; there are vibrations of sympathy and antipathy.[18]

Rudolf Steiner goes on to say that sympathy is a brief falling
asleep in which we 'sleepingly' investigate the Ego of the other.
We wake up in the antipathy phase and transfer to our awareness what we have perceived in sleep, and so experience the
other person and recognize them as a being.

Unconsciously there are two things that we want: As Ego
beings we want to exert an influence on others. But we also want
to experience who the other person is, because by doing so we
can measure ourselves against the other and thus learn something about ourselves.

We will now turn to descriptions given by Rudolf Steiner in
which he speaks about individuals who have no Ego *from birth*,
who therefore are genuinely egoless individuals not subject to
the law of reincarnation and karma.

An egoless girl discussed by Rudolf Steiner at a teachers' meeting of the Waldorf School

We begin with a case discussed by Rudolf Steiner at a teachers' meeting[19] of the Waldorf School in Stuttgart (on 3 July 1923). It concerned a girl in the first class, L.W., who was unable to absorb any lesson content because she was initially focused only on herself and constantly disturbed the lesson.

These are cases occurring more and more frequently where children are born and human forms exist which are actually not human with respect to the higher Ego, but are occupied by beings not belonging to the category of human. Since the 'nineties {of the nineteenth century} there have been many egoless people who have no {sequence of} reincarnations, but where the human form is filled out by a kind of nature demon. There are already large numbers of people going about who are actually not human beings but are nature-spirit beings who are human only in form.

A teacher asks: How is this possible?

Rudolf Steiner:

It is not out of the question that a miscalculation happens in the cosmos. The descending individualities are determined for each other long beforehand. There are also generations into which no individuality wants to descend and unite with a bodily nature, or they immediately leave the body. Then other individualities step in who don't fit properly. [...] They are very different from human beings with regard to their mental abilities. For example they can never commit to memory anything that is in sentences. They only have word memory, not sentence memory.

The enigma of life is not simple. When such a being passes through death, it goes back to nature where it came from. The corpse decomposes; there is not a proper dissolution of the etheric body, and the being goes back into nature.[20]

Stefan Leber, a lecturer at the Seminar for Waldorf Pedagogy in Stuttgart, outlined this case in an article in the *Lehrer-Rundbrief*[21] (Teachers' Newsletter).

> The child in question was a girl in the first class who could only be managed if the teacher, Frau Dr. Bettina Mellinger, held her hand; otherwise she constantly bit, scratched and kicked those around her. This extreme behaviour was the reason for bringing the subject of the child to the teachers' meeting. And it seemed obvious where the discussion would lead, namely that the child could not be carried in the class. Also, from things Rudolf Steiner was saying [...], one could assume that it was a matter of excluding the child from the school. Nothing could be farther from the truth! Steiner's explanation clarified the girl's destiny situation in order, through understanding, to convey to the colleagues, and primarily to the teacher most 'affected', {the importance of} taking on the task that presented itself to them, and keeping the girl at the school. Rudolf Steiner himself apparently gazed at the girl for a long time, stroked her head, and after this there was a marked improvement in her behaviour. This task was taken up so intensively that the girl remained in the school for eight years.

The young woman afterwards did a variety of simple jobs. Later on she married, but always suffered from severe depression. 'When I once visited the nearly 70-year-old woman,' Leber writes, 'it was clear that the school was a place with which she felt connected with good memories.'

Many questions arise when we consider there are people who do not have an Ego and yet live as human beings in a human form.

One question we can ask is: Do these egoless people also have an angel who guides them? We feel impelled to answer this question in the affirmative—even if we are unable to answer all the secondary questions that arise from this 'yes'.

But we can say the following: Lydia was led to the Waldorf school, to her teacher, and to Rudolf Steiner who gave her his spiritual strength and thereby stabilized her.

The following text comes from an obituary of Bettina Mellinger:

> There was a momentous occasion when Rudolf Steiner inter-
> vened and put the teacher to a hard test. She had a girl in her
> class who was extremely wild. She was also usually covered in
> dirt from head to toe from crawling about in all the corners. For
> years the child could not be induced to take part in the lesson.
> Bettina Mellinger also noticed that she never cried. When she
> visited the parents, she found them living in the direst circum-
> stances. She gave the girl a doll which was soon lying in the cor-
> ner with its head cut off. One evening when the child was going
> to bed, {Bettina Mellinger} came and gave her a picture of 'The
> Madonna with Child' by Fra Lippo Lippi. There for the first time
> she observed how, with fixed eyes, the child was able to pause for
> a moment with concentration, calm and stillness of soul. She then
> awaited Rudolf Steiner's visit to Stuttgart in order to hear his
> advice, but when he entered the classroom the child was absent.
> She was often away and had to be fetched on this day as well.
> When she was brought, unwashed, to Rudolf Steiner, he looked
> at her lovingly and took her arm, whereupon she burst into tears.
> Astonished, Rudolf Steiner asked, 'Does she often cry?' 'No, not
> at all.' He gave some instruction on what to do, and the lesson
> continued. There was no change in the girl's behaviour until a
> dramatic incident occurred.
>
> There was a singing lesson going on, and the child had been
> left in the classroom with the door locked because she was unable
> to sing with the others and the singing teacher couldn't deal with
> the disruptions any more. Then her classmates in the music room
> saw the girl hanging from the outside window sill of the first-
> floor window. Instantly horrified, Bettina Mellinger bolted to the
> classroom and pulled the child in. After that the girl's behaviour
> was good again. She had no notion of danger and seemed to be
> only half human.
>
> The girl then went into Dr Schubert's remedial class. When
> Rudolf Steiner next visited the class the first thing he asked was,

'Where is our worrisome child?' 'In the remedial class. I myself and the subject teachers couldn't take the responsibility any more.' Whereupon Rudolf Steiner said, 'This child belongs with you and in your class!'

Bettina Mellinger often had to hold the restless girl's hand and walk up and down with her while teaching. Once she had got to grips with this task, discipline in the rest of the class was no longer a problem. In further conversation with Rudolf Steiner it was clear that this was a case beyond usual pedagogical measures; something had to be made good by pedagogical and medicinal means which is otherwise done for the human being, with regard to his spiritual being, by the Spirits of Form. This circumstance awoke a new enthusiasm for teaching in Bettina Mellinger. The girl grew into a decent individual; the teacher had found her formative force.[22]

The question of egoless individuals in Rudolf Steiner's discussions with the priests of the Christian Community

Rudolf Steiner had not wanted the lectures given to the priests to be generally accessible. 'Apart from this circle, only members of the Executive Committee of the Goetheanum [*Vorstand*] were present,' he wrote in an article for the members' newsletter, where he mentions this course.[23] He covered the subject of egoless individuals who would appear in the future and are described in a stupendous imagination in the Apocalypse of St John. We will look at Lecture 13 of the course for priests.[24] In this lecture Rudolf Steiner explains the *plague of locusts* described in Revelation, Chapter 9:

> In appearance the locusts are like horses armed for battle. They appear to be wearing gold crowns on their heads, and their faces are like human faces. They have hair like women's hair, and their teeth are like those of lions. They have armour like breastplates of iron, and the sound of their wings is like the clatter of chariots of war drawn by many galloping horses. They have tails and stings like scorpions, and their power to bring disaster upon mankind for five months lies in their tails. As their king they have the angel of the abyss leading them, whose name is Abaddon in Hebrew, Apollyon in Greek.[25]

We can outline some of the spiritual researcher's statements as follows: The angel of the abyss is a high ahrimanic being. The locusts are an imagination for egoless people.

> [...] a kind of surplus of individuals is appearing in our times who are without Egos, who are not truly human beings. This is a terrible truth. They walk about {but} they are not an incarnation of an Ego; they are placed in the physical line of heredity, receive an etheric body and astral body, {but} in a certain sense are fitted out with an ahrimanic consciousness. They make the impression of a

human being if we do not look closely, but they are not human in the fullest sense of the word.[26]

A weakening of the Ego, to the point of egolessness, comes about today through computer addiction. An alien power that wants nothing more than to live in the virtual world gets hold of the person slumped in front of the monitor.

What is working on the psyche here has a locust nature, eating everything bare and empty and destroying the will that comes from the Ego.

Rudolf Steiner now addresses the priests—the priest is a carer of souls:

> [The priest] must also be able to find the words for everything that is going on in these souls. They most definitely *do not always have to be evil souls; they can be souls that get as far as a soul nature but lack an Ego* [italics by E.G.]. The priest needs to know this, for this influences the quality of the community between people. Above all, people who are properly ensouled suffer through such individuals who actually go through the world as human locusts. And the question arises, and must arise: How do we relate to such people?
>
> We often have a difficult task when faced with people like this, because they [egoless individuals, E.G.] are very much people of deep feeling; [...] but we notice there is no proper individuality inside them. Naturally we must be careful not to reveal to them that they have no individuality, for this would inevitably lead to insanity. Despite having to hide this from them, we need to arrange things for these souls—for they are indeed souls even though not spirits—so that they make contact with other people in whose society they can develop, that they become fellow travellers in a certain sense of these others. These people evince fairly precisely the characteristics and nature of the individual up to the age of 20. For it is in the twentieth year of life that the mind-soul or intellectual-soul is born, making it possible for the Ego to express itself in earthly life.

Anyone wanting to maintain that there is no need to relate sympathetically towards these egoless people, these people without an individuality, since they will not have a future incarnation because there is no individuality there, would be greatly mistaken. They would then also have to maintain that we should not relate sympathetically towards children. When it comes to deciding what is actually in such a person, each case must be looked at separately. Sometimes there are posthumous souls in these people, posthumous in contrast to human souls that arose at a particular era of evolution and have incarnated repeatedly as human beings. But they can also be souls that remained behind, souls that returned later from another planet to which almost all of humanity had gone during a particular epoch. Souls of that nature can also be in such people. With full consciousness we need to nurture these people like individuals who remain children.[27]

We can summarize Rudolf Steiner's statements to the priests with reference to the Apocalypse, concerning egoless people:

- There are egoless people who have an *ahrimanic consciousness*, i.e. that are possessed by an ahrimanic being.
- Egoless people are *not necessarily evil.*
- Without an ego, they can be people with *deep feelings.*
- They can develop in soul if they make contact with human beings endowed with an Ego.
- Egoless people should not learn they have no Ego. This would cause them to go mad.
- In connection with this: The depressions suffered by Lydia were a precursor to the above-mentioned madness.
- Egoless people express the nature that everyone has up to the age of 20.
- They remain at this more childish stage of their development. They should be treated with empathy.

- Sometimes there are posthumous souls in these people. These are souls that have remained behind, who stayed for a long time on another planet and only incarnated on Earth very late.
- Before the moon's withdrawal from the earth in the Lemurian age, the *whole of humanity* had removed to other cosmic localities in order to await more favourable conditions for their evolution on earth.

Anthroposophists wishing to work actively will train themselves in recognizing egolessness so as to be able in the future apocalyptic times to help where help will be necessary.

The effect of cyanide on bodily processes involved with the will

We learn from anthroposophy that the spiritual and physical principles interpenetrate one another, or, more precisely, that there is an interplay between the forces of spirit and of matter, particularly when we move our physical body.

Our movement as human beings is actually a magical working that entails something being set in motion by spirit.

The will, which is purely spiritual, must reach into physical activity. This is a magical process. When you walk, your inner magician is at work; he is something very real. How does this happen? We are not mobile beings because we are made of bones, blood and so on; with these we could at most be a resting being, a being eternally lying in bed, but not a moving being. For {in order for movement to occur} the will must be directly involved. Materialistic science is making things easy for itself with the theory of motor nerves and so on. This is nonsensical. In reality what we have when we carry out a movement is a magical effect, a direct intervention of the spirit into our bodily movements.

How is this possible?

It comes about as follows: I mentioned this afternoon that when we go from our rhythmic system towards our metabolic and limbic system, the changes in carbon begin to show their affinity with the changes in nitrogen, and a constant tendency arises down below in us to create compounds of carbon and nitrogen. This tendency exists. We will not be able to understand the digestive process, and particularly the excretion process, until we look at the tendency of carbon to form compounds with nitrogen. This tendency of carbon and nitrogen to form compounds results finally in the formation of cyanic acid; so there is in the human being the constant tendency to generate cyanic acid or salts of cyanide. We don't even have a proper term for what arises here.

What arises is pushed only to the point of *beginning* to arise, then, through secretions from the gall bladder, the process is suspended. So in our lower regions we have a tendency to produce cyanide compounds which are stopped *in status nascendi* by gall bladder secretions. The production of cyanide compounds in the human being would mean the human being's destruction. The quickest way to destroy the human structure is to permeate it with cyanide. But this tendency does actually exist as we approach the limbic and metabolic system. The human organism is constantly trying to produce cyanide compounds which are immediately destroyed again. But it is in this moment between the production and the immediate dissolution of the cyanide compounds that the will can enter and engage our system of muscles.

The paralysing of this process gives the will the opportunity to take hold so that the human being can move. Towards our lower organism there is a constant tendency to destroy organic substance by poisoning. It is perpetually at a beginning stage, and we could not move, we could not attain to freedom of will, if we did not have this constant tendency to destroy ourselves. So, putting it rather grotesquely, towards our lower organism we have a constant tendency to turn ourselves into ghosts, and thereby to move ourselves magically. We should not look to the physical body {to explain how} people walk about but to their will, to the eliciting of movements in space through purely magical means.[28]

Let us see if we can get a better understanding of these statements.

Steiner speaks about how the will, which is something of a purely spiritual nature, can have an effect in our muscles which gives rise to movements in the physical body. These do not arise through the motor nerves, as Steiner remarks, but are activated magically.

Someone with a scientific training might well recoil at the mention of 'magic', fearing a sliding back into a 'pre-scientific' age. The opposite is the case. Steiner presents the findings of his research which scientific thinking has yet to catch up with.

This will happen when we are able to overcome our materialistic thinking.

Steiner says that, 'going downwards'—that is, in the lower regions of the body—there is a tendency to produce salts of cyanide which, however, are dissolved as they arise since otherwise the body would be destroyed.

A process in the lower organism—in our metabolic-limbic system—must stand in contrast to a process in the upper organism—in our rhythmic and nerve-sense system:

> Whereas carbon has a tendency lower down to form nitrogen compounds, so it has the tendency going upwards [in the physical body, E.G.] to form oxygen compounds. The early alchemists called it 'the stone of the wise'; this is nothing other than the full understanding of carbon. It has the tendency going upwards to form oxygen compounds, oxygen acids or oxygen salts. These stimulate thoughts, and every time we occupy the child in a lively pictorial way, we stimulate the production of carbonic acid and therefore the thinking.[29]

We learn from Steiner that we need to understand the action of chemical elements 'morally'.

Oxygen stimulates thoughts. In other words, this element has a positive effect on the nerve-sense system.

'Every time we get the child not just to think but at the same time to do something, we bring about a balance between the formation of carbonic acid and the production of cyanide. And it is very important in life that these two things are produced equally.'[30]

If you have been following so far, you may be asking how the matter covered in this chapter is connected with the theme of egoless people.

The connection is cyanogen which, like a leitmotif, brings the reader's thoughts in touch with all the incidents and situations in which cyanogen is involved.

The task and effect of comets

In a course on the Apocalypse held at the Goetheanum from 12 to 22 September 1924 for the priests of the newly-forming Christian Community, Rudolf Steiner speaks about the nature of comets and the task they have had and still have.

When the writer of the Apocalypse speaks about comets, he does so by presenting them in an Imagination of animal forms.

In the cosmos, planets are heavenly bodies whose motions follow a regular course. Their movements can thus be calculated. The course of comets, by contrast, is 'moody', i.e. sometimes they cross the orbit of planets and sometimes they don't. These processes were observed and discussed with great interest. The intersection of the path of comets with the orbits of planets was followed by the wider public with concern and fear. Many people thought comet collisions with the earth would lead to the earth's destruction. Steiner discusses a particular comet—Biela's Comet—for which {doom-laden} calculations of this nature had been made:

> The day arrived—I can still remember very well the anxious expectation everywhere—and lo and behold, the comet didn't appear at all! In its place there was the most wonderfully beautiful, magnificent meteor shower. A really wonderful meteor shower, like a night fire falling to earth from the sky in a spray of myriad sparks. The comet had first split in two and then broken up into many tiny fragments that could be absorbed by the earth's atmosphere, that were united with the earth's being. [The comet] had taken the path of being absorbed by the earth.[31]

Steiner talks here about a *meteor shower* that had arisen from the disintegration of comet substance. There is a strong relationship between the two.

Later on the spiritual teacher talks about the comet events of the year 1933. Calculations were predicting a catastrophe in 1933.

In other words, if the comet did not split by then, a catastrophe would definitely ensue where:

> all the seas would cover the earth in gigantic floods destroying all life on earth. But the comet has already dissolved, it is absorbed as particles by the earth, the earth nourishes itself from this cosmic substance. And instead of there being a collision in 1933—and we are not far away from it [1924]—what the earth has already absorbed will be spiritualized by other substances, and the spiritual element will rise up. The earth digests the comets, the spiritual rises up. My dear friends, a comet principle now spiritualized (*vergeistigtes Kometarisches*) thus rises up from the earth from time to time.[32]

What does Steiner say about the task of comets? In short: the earth 'digests' comets.

> If there were no comets we would not have been able to withstand the demands made on our physical body by way of the astral body, if this astral body, which constitutes the animal nature in human beings, were not constantly being remediated, undergoing a real therapy, by that which, through the absorbed comet substance, is radiated back to the surface of the earth and has a balancing effect on human faculties.[33]

'Digested' comet forces are the remediation for the animal aspect of the astral body; without this corrective influence the physical body could not cope with the astral body.

Let us go more deeply into the esoteric side of comets:

> Now just consider this matter, my dear friends, in the great context of the cosmos. The earth consumes comet substance and gives it back in spiritualized form which unites with human astral bodies in both a good and an evil sense. We see comets in the skies during a particular epoch, but where are they after this epoch? In a lecture in Paris in 1906 I mentioned—at a time when external science was a long way from discussing it, but discovered it later through spectrum analysis—that the substance of comets

contained cyanogen, compounds of carbon and nitrogen. This is of great significance, for cyan, distributed in tiny amounts on the earth, is needed to purify astral bodies. A tremendously significant doctor is at work in the cosmos who carries out treatments of this nature more or less continuously. Just think: What is seen in the skies during a particular epoch atomizes, as I described; it falls from the sky as a fiery shower, later on it is in the soil, and later still it migrates from the soil into plants, into roots, stems, leaves, and blossoms. We eat this comet content, this comet ferment, given by the cosmos to the earth—we eat it in our bread. The writer of the Apocalypse sees this phenomenon: a spirituality rises up with beneficial effects from one comet and with adverse effects from another. The beast will be loose from its imprisonment in the earth—in cosmic terms this is the comet. The beast will be loose—this has significance for the evolution of humanity. This directs us to very powerful realities, to points of great significance for the development of humankind on earth.

In 1933, my dear friends, there would be the possibility of the earth and every living thing on it being destroyed were it not for the existence of another wise measure which cannot be calculated. The fact is that calculations can no longer get it right once a comet has taken on a different form. We would have to say, in terms of the writer of the Apocalypse: Before the etheric Christ can be understood in the right way by human beings, humanity must first deal with an encounter with the beast that rises up in 1933.[34]

The beast that rose up in 1933 can be understood as the force behind Adolf Hitler and National Socialism {Nazism}, and comes to expression as an impulse of Sorat.[35] This impulse rises up out of the earth. And humanity has to face it. In other words, it has to conquer this and similar worldviews.

Then the atmosphere will be free, and the etheric Christ, who is always present, can be experienced and apprehended by people.

As mentioned above, cyanogen, present in minute quantities in comet material, has a harmonizing effect on wild astrality in human beings.

In the chapter on the magical intervention of the will in activating bodily movement, the spiritual researcher emphasized how this happens only momentarily and that cyanogen immediately disappears again.

When potassium cyanide is used in sufficiently high dosage to kill people—as happened in Auschwitz and other concentration camps—*a destruction of the Ego* occurs that can only be overcome through the helping and healing power of the hierarchies.

Sorat

Sorat {or Sorath} is the horned beast of the Apocalypse. He is the Sun Demon; as such he is the direct adversary of Christ who is the Spirit of the Sun and also, through the Mystery of Golgotha, the Spirit of the Earth.

Sorat has an occult symbol which expresses his nature.

He is a being originating from other cosmic periods, and has appropriated the tendencies of these other periods. Sorat is deeply satisfied when he finds human individuals who have refused to receive what the human being can attain through life and activity on earth: namely, the *Christ impulse.*

> He [Sorat] saw the coming evolution of the earth, but said to himself: I have not advanced sufficiently far with the earth that I could get something from earthly existence. This being could only have got something from the earth if it had been able to gain rulership at a particular moment: namely, when the Christ Principle descended to earth. If this Christ Principle had been stifled in its beginnings at that time, if the adversary had been able to overcome Christ, then indeed it would have been possible for the earth in its totality to fall to this Sorat Principle. This didn't

happen; and so this being had to be satisfied with the left-overs that have not inclined towards the Christ Principle, with those human individuals who have remained stuck in matter. They will be his hosts in the future.[36]

Sorat uses Lucifer and Ahriman as his accomplices, and lures people into black magic. The number of Sorat is 666. This must signify the principle that brings human beings to a total hardening in outer physical life, so that they literally expel from themselves that which enables them to shed their lower nature and ascend to their higher. What the human being has received as his physical and lower ego-nature before he raises himself up to the higher Ego, what he has received in these four principles is expressed in four {Hebrew} letters: the physical body in *samech*, the etheric body in *waw*, the astral body in *resh*, and the lower ego in *taw*. As a Hebrew word, 'Sorat' is read from right to left.

Rudolf Steiner speaks about the mystery secrets in the word 'Sorat'. It is a matter of understanding the occult significance of the sounds and numbers and how these relate. For the time being, however, it will be enough to bear in mind that the word 'Sorat' gives the human being forces which lead him to a total hardening in outer physical life.

> People will already have begun to assimilate this disposition to descend into the abyss in the far distant future, after the great war of all against all in the age [of the trumpets] when the seventh trumpet sounds. However, for a long time it will still be possible for individuals who have absorbed this disposition to come back, to revert and return in their development in order still to take up the Christ principle. But the first predisposition will have begun, and those who remain with it will, when that far distant future comes that is indicated not by 466 but by 666, no longer be able to change this into a good disposition. They will face the terrible destiny of which we still need to speak.[37]

So the spiritual researcher states that today a materialistic person still has time to change. Nevertheless temptations and enticements will come that develop the materialistic predisposition still further. And when 6 great and 6 smaller time periods have passed, after 66, there will already be very concerning tendencies in humanity which will not be as easy to put right as in our time.

The *law of karma* has been mentioned a number of times in this book. According to this law we do not live once but return from the spiritual world in many reincarnations on earth.

Why?

Because the law of humanity is one of *evolution*. We have the stupendous opportunity in each life to develop further. But this is only possible *on the earth*. This is where we can rectify our mistakes. In the period between death and a new birth, we work, together with higher spirit-beings, on shaping our future life. We therefore have a *life-plan* which we bring with us into our new life. In our daily awareness we know nothing of this. But at night when we sleep, we submerse ourselves once more in this plan— or more precisely, in our *karma*.

And we know in the depths of our soul what this karma wants of us, even if we hesitate in acting on it in life.

We might have the impression from these few indications that everything in life is predetermined; but for many things karma gives us space. It lies within the freedom of the individual how this space is filled. But there are events in life that are not determined by karma, such as car accidents, volcanic eruptions, floods, or earthquakes.

What does a materialistic person experience who is catapulted out of their physical body by a car accident? *They experience the reality of the spiritual world*. Due to the accident they suddenly find themself in the spiritual world they did not believe in, but which they now actually experience. The important point now is whether this individual is able to process their life spiritually. This means, whether they are able to understand and accept the law of karma; whether they can comprehend the spiritual aspect of their relationships with others; whether they recognize their *life motif*.

This individual experiences the challenge from the spiritual world to raise themself up to spirit—that is, to accept spirit as an organizing power. And they say to themself: 'So there *is* a supersensory world after all.' If they accept this realization, the individual can reincarnate quickly. But, if they wish to understand the workings of the spiritual world in their life, they must become a seeker of the spirit. This means that, if they reincarnate quickly, they become an inquirer, one who looks for the relation between the spiritual world and higher spirit-beings. But a speedy reincarnation is not always beneficial. Someone who has lived entirely materialistically enters a spiritual darkness after death. In this situation they are not able to receive the gifts offered by higher spiritual beings. But these gifts are needed by the soul in the period between death and rebirth to shape one's future karma. By living a life of entirely materialistic thoughts, we finally lose our connection to morality. There are people who ask why they should act and be morally good: 'Why should I be good and kind when other people aren't?' they could ask.

When we hear a question like this, we understand someone thinks in this way because their feeling life is weak. Someone, on the other hand, who faces their destiny, experiences how accepting their life-circumstances—that is, their karma—gives them the deepest satisfaction.

Life is a school in which we also have to experience difficult times. But we become strong through our experiences, if we gain in *self-knowledge.*

The situation prior to the First World War

At this juncture we will allow ourselves a digression, but connected with our theme, and take a look at the English historian Niall Ferguson (born 1964). He wrote a book, very worth the read, with the title *The Pity of War*.[38] In this book Ferguson demonstrates that the First World War was based on fallacious premises and wrong decisions on the part of all the decision-makers.

For years before the outbreak of the war the countries that would later be involved in waging it were pervaded by public opinion hostile to all 'the others'. This gave rise to a superficial and prejudiced form of literature that produced many novels and reports about exposing spies.

The most influential novel was published in 1909—William Le Queux's *Spies of the Kaiser*, about a network of German spies in the island kingdom. Captain Henry Curties' *When England Slept* was published at the same time. In this novel, London is occupied overnight by a German army which in the course of a few weeks had invaded the British kingdom unnoticed.

Ernest Oldmeadow's novel *North Sea Bubble* (1906) even describes how the Germans attempted to win over their new vassals by distributing Christmas presents and subsidized food. Indeed, the worst atrocity the occupying forces subjected their victims to was the introduction of a new food regime consisting largely of German-style wurst and sauerkraut. In addition, the Germans saw to it that the name 'Handel' was printed properly in concert programmes as 'Händel'.

The Germans too produced visions of future wars in novels of a similar level to the English ones. For example, Karl Eisenhart's *Die Abrechnung mit England* (Settling the account with England) (1900); or Paul Georg Mönch's *Hindenburgs Einmarsch in London* (Hindenburg's march into London), published in 1915, which describes a successful invasion over the English Channel by the victor from Tannenberg. The impression we get from Niall

Ferguson's list of books, even without reading them, is enough to suggest to us that everything depicted in this 'war literature' generated a pervasive mood of hatred among the British, French, and German populations, which would inevitably result in Hitler's evil deeds in Germany. Here too the adage applies: thoughts create reality.

In 1916 Rudolf Steiner indicated that inside the circle of English Lodges, a war with Germany had already been decided upon in 1888.[39]

Ceremonial magic—the technique
of occult Lodges

In the lecture cycle *In geänderter Zeitlage*[40] (In the changed situation of the times), Rudolf Steiner tries to give his audience an understanding of the background to historical events. Through anthroposophy a complete renewal of cultural civilization became possible, which could lead people into spiritual freedom. Spiritual matters were no longer to remain abstract, but were to flow concretely into culture through spiritual research, so that a bridge could be built in science, the arts, and religion, from the sensory world to the supersensory.

This impulse inevitably came up against opposition from powers that did not wish to allow people an independent spiritual development out of inner freedom.

There are Lodges and sects that do not serve human progress. They want to prevent a breakthrough to the spirit, the overcoming of materialism, and a culture founded on spiritual freedom. In this wish many different secret societies in both East and West coincide. A leading role is played here by the Anglo-Saxon occult Lodges. Their objective, among other things, is to establish a world empire of Americanism.

This is not to say anything against the many positive ideas and aspirations that come from England and America. Every nation and culture has a positive mission. Recognizing and absorbing this is a task every spiritual student gladly undertakes because they know that without the deepening and enrichment that comes from such an acquaintance, they would become one-sided and not be able to reach their spiritual goals.

Working out of the spirit, which is what spiritual students dedicate themselves to, is always connected with a positive relation to all cultures, all languages, and the spirit of each nation.

What is presented here as the statements of the spiritual researcher is not intended to criticize the nature of any nation or culture, but to turn our attention to the problematic *occult powers* that work behind the scenes and set up spiritual hindrances. The question is whether, in their everyday consciousness, national leaders are aware of the plans of these occult Lodges or not.

In the lecture series mentioned above, *In geänderter Zeitlage*, the spiritual researcher speaks about the plans and objectives of these Western Lodges. He makes reference to individuals who were alive at the time. With regard to this question, he says the politicians were barely aware of these plans. 'You therefore don't need to ask whether Northcliffe or even Lloyd George[41] were initiated into this or that grade of the forces involved here. That is not what's important. What *is* important is whether it is possible for them to act in the interests of these forces. They only need to absorb the tendency of these forces into their instincts. This is possible, however; it happens.'[42]

How is an influence of this nature brought about? What techniques do the Lodges use?

Rudolf Steiner gives just an indication of this when he says the following: 'You see, occult societies of this kind want a great deal. Among other things—we can only describe single details, they want a lot more—they want the following: they want in a certain sense to over-materialize materialism; they want to create more materialism in the world than would naturally arise in the course of human evolution.'

How do the Lodges do this? By using 'ceremonial magic'.

'Now, the characteristic of certain kinds of ceremonial magic is that they really [...] have a certain effect on the physical apparatus of people. [...] A spiritual element that arises through the influence of certain operations of ceremonial magic can work into [...] the system of ganglia, into the spinal cord system.' When people participate in meetings in which ceremonies take place which have the effect just described, then:

> the possibility is created for those who have died, among other spirits, to exert an influence on the people entangled in such a circle as is created by ceremonial magic. But through this, my dear friends, the materialism of our time can be 'over-materialized' in

a certain sense. Imagine someone who is entirely materialistically minded, not only in their worldview but also in all their sensibilities, in their feeling—and there are a huge number of people like this in the West. Their material-mindedness is then amplified to a still higher degree. The person then feels a compulsion to influence the material world not only while they are still living in a physical body but also beyond death. What they strive for is: 'When I die, I want to have some locus through which I can exert an influence on people still living, whom I have left behind on the earth, or who are trained for me.' There are people in our times whose urge towards materialism is so strong that they look for some arrangement through which they can still influence things in the material world beyond their death. And such instruments through which people ensure a material dominance beyond death, are the locations of certain ceremonial magic.[43]

Thus it is a matter of exercising power on the physical plane. This is applied in such a way as to block a renewal of culture beyond materialism.

No spiritual freedom, no spiritualization, no independent spiritual seeking—this is what is to be achieved, these are the watchwords of the underground leadership of the spiritual climate.

Someone who is strengthened by the power impulses of such deceased people, and who works in politics, radiates a suggestive power which, in their speeches, in their newspaper articles, in the way they talk to people, has the effect that their will and their objectives are absorbed into the subconscious of their contemporaries. Thus, through this assistance from beyond the threshold of death, a magical power can be exerted over others.

People who have got into 'super-materialism' in this way, seek an ahrimanic immortality, not, however, in the spiritual sphere, but in the physical. For these people, 'the society they have joined is the guarantor that forces of theirs will live on beyond death which should actually only live to the point of their physical death. [...] There are societies today which—conceived spiritually, conceived occultly—are 'insurance companies' for ahrimanic immortality.[44]

> It is always only a small number of individuals who are aware of all these things, for as a rule societies such as these are organized so that the ceremonial magic has an effect particularly on those who have no idea, on people who have a certain need to have a relationship with the spiritual world through all sorts of symbolic rituals. There are many people like this. It is truly not the worst people who want this. These people are accepted into a circle of ceremonial magic. Within this there is a small group of individuals who use the others who have entered the ceremonial magic circle, actually as their instruments.[45]

One should therefore treat with caution all so-called occult societies that have so-called higher grades whose objectives are kept secret from the lower grades.

The leaders of secret societies seek to make effective in an occult way the spiritual forces of their deceased predecessors. These want to continue to operate in the earthly sphere from the realm of the dead and thus attain a material immortality. The unconscious soul-sphere of the living, who participate as brother Lodge members in the ceremonies in question, are influenced in this way and used for the purposes of the Lodges. But through this the Lodge brothers open themselves up to a further occult influence coming to them from particular spiritual beings. Every human being has a positive, helping relationship to their angelos. However, ever since the Egypto-Chaldaean era there have been angeloi who have remained behind and become ahrimanic. The participants in ceremonial magic now become connected also to these angeloi.

> And these retrograde angeloi, as I have described for you, play a large part in such occult societies: they are important helpers and important directing spirits. Thus there is much in these occult societies that is intent on transposing aspects of Egyptian-Chaldaean times onto the present. When this is not just frippery [...]

but is really involved in occult life, it happens under the influence of retrograde beings of the hierarchy of angeloi, who are the leaders here. And thus we have also pointed to beings of the closest supersensory hierarchy {to us}, who are sought out by these societies.[46]

By these means the Lodges attain strong magical power. It manifests, among other things, in the ability to give the stamp of truth to what is untrue.

'And it is indeed a magical operation, an important magical operation, to spread what is untrue in such a way in the world that it works like the truth, for there is an enormous force of evil in this working of untruth.'[47]

The occult forces emanating from these Lodges, as mentioned above, operate even into the instincts of politicians who open themselves psychologically to these impulses.

In connection with what has just been discussed concerning occult Lodges, there is another question to consider: *hatred of Germany*, of German culture and the German language. Rudolf Steiner does not go into this, but mentions two individuals in British political life who were also participants in ceremonial magic: Northcliffe and Lloyd George.

Viscount Alfred Northcliffe, 1865-1922, was a journalist and newspaper magnate. Even before the First World War he directed polemic attacks against Germany. During the conflict he organized a smear campaign against Germany's conduct of the war. Northcliffe was a life-long opponent of anything German.

Lloyd George, 1863-1945, became a minister in 1909, and Prime Minister from 1917 to 1922. He preached the complete 'knock out' of the German Reich. At the 1919 peace conference in Paris, he supported placing the whole guilt for the war on Germany.[48]

We mentioned above that every nation has its mission. It is carried and inspired by its folk-spirit. The folk-spirit is a spiritual being of the hierarchies. Every nation has its own folk-spirit, of archangel rank, which inspires suitable individuals of the nation with its mission.

The task of the German folk-spirit is to translate soul experience into an understanding of ideas. In other words: Germans have the ability to experience ideas {as such} in their soul. In this experience they unconsciously cross the threshold to the spiritual world.

But ideas need words in order to grasp and communicate them. This is why the spiritual researcher Rudolf Steiner needed the body of the language of the Central European people to enable him to incarnate his work, anthroposophy.

He looked with concern to the future, where there is a tendency to disable the German folk-spirit. This objective was something secret societies were already working towards at the end of the nineteenth century. In his *Zeitgeschichtliche Betrachtungen*, the spiritual researcher mentioned that the First World War could have broken out in 1888. Already at that time measures were being taken to prevent the spiritual-scientific contribution Germany was called on to perform, as mentioned earlier.[49]

Rudolf Steiner summarized his concern for Germany in the following mantric words which he spoke in Berlin on 14 January 1915:[50]

> The German Spirit has not yet completed
> What it is meant to achieve in world-becoming.
> Full of hope, it lives with future concern,
> Full of life, it hopes for future deeds;
> In the depths of its being it powerfully feels
> Something hidden, which, still maturing, must take effect.
> How can the wish for its demise arise
> In enemy power lacking understanding,
> So long as the life is revealed to it
> Which, creating, holds it in its being's roots?

When we read and meditate on this mantra, the question arises: *Who is Rudolf Steiner* that he is able to utter such words which can express the spiritual situation of the nations engaged in the world war, and thereby have a helpful influence?

To cover the spiritual stature of Rudolf Steiner comprehensively would require the writing of other books. Let the statement suffice that the *masters*[51] work with and through Rudolf Steiner, and that we participate spiritually when we meditate on this mantra.

It was no accident that Rudolf Steiner incarnated into the sphere of German culture. For, what is the contribution German culture can make towards the common development of humanity? It consists in *taking up anthroposophy*. The German language is particularly suited to this. It is flexible but nevertheless possesses a strong formative power. Both are needed when spiritual content is to be encapsulated and understood in language and concepts. Language that is suitable for earthly things has to become a vessel for supersensory content.

A person who follows this content in thought takes steps in thinking which lead them over the threshold into the spiritual world.

The question arises here: If the Germans are so gifted at absorbing spiritual content, why did such masses of them become supporters of Hitler and members of the Nazi Party?

The answer is: they let themselves be seduced by Hitler's being.

As discussed above, Hitler was an empty shell; there was no human Ego living in him. Hitler was a servant of Sorat; his corporeal and human form, during phases of possession by the sun demon Sorat, had an enormously powerful effect. Even great American magnates were admirers and supporters of Hitler.[52] This effect was carefully prepared in the Western Lodges by ensuring that the successor-state to the German Kaiser Reich, the Weimar Republic, would not succeed—we need only think of the crushing war reparations the German people were required to pay, the French occupation of the Rhineland and Saarland that followed the guilt for the war being laid solely on Germany. We should also not forget the enormous financial support given to Hitler by American banks, and a great deal more.

It was easy for Hitler in his public speeches to criticize these measures and humiliating conditions, and to awaken in his audiences the expectation that everything bad at that time due to losing the war could at a stroke be turned into 'good' by him, Hitler.

Added to this was the expulsion of Jews from German society, to the point of killing millions with potassium cyanide. People would have had to be much firmer of character to be able to withstand these seductions. The situation that was 'incarnated' in the most evil way into German life by Hitler and his aides, was also directed against anthroposophy and its daughter-movements (like anthroposophical medicine, biodynamic agriculture, and the Waldorf schools), which were banned and defamed.

After the end of the Second World War the members of the Anthroposophical Society were able to build up and carry out what they had been prohibited from doing by National Socialism. And it became evident that the seed of spiritual science had been sown in fertile soil.

But it was not only German anthroposophists who worked in this way: all the cultures and languages over the whole globe were working on this renewal of human culture. It was a matter of *overcoming materialism* and shaping life on spiritual foundations.

An American sect

We will now look at a widely spread sect which, however, being established only after Steiner's death, was not mentioned by him. It can serve here as an example of the working of Western, American sects. We are referring to the Church of Scientology, founded by science-fiction writer Lafayette Ronald Hubbard (1911-1986).

The methods employed by Hubbard and his successors are intended to lead people to the point where they free themselves from all psychological-personal and destiny-related connections.

What do the members of this 'church' want? They are preparing a new culture. For this they have to be 'clean': this means they should free themselves from everything that oppresses them psychologically and from all the undigested problems they carry around with them. To achieve this the member has to buy and complete an expensive series of courses. If they don't have enough money, they can borrow—even to the point of bankruptcy. Members who want to leave this 'church' are persecuted and threatened, as credibly reported by former members.

We are inclined to see in Hubbard an egoless leader with a strong ahrimanic effect and influence, who neither wanted nor was able, psychologically or physically, to let the members go. 'Respect for people's freedom,' however, is the magical phrase that needs to be alive in all co-operative spiritual work and aspiration. Where this is not the case, it is not possible for a new culture to arise from the work, even though this is what Hubbard proclaimed as the objective of his 'church'. Raising money from members does, however, make for a financially powerful worldwide enterprise.

We can ask another question: Is Hubbard also one of the deceased who from beyond the threshold can exert an influence on the still-living members with the help of ceremonial magic, even though Hubbard is a being without a human Ego?

We consider we have to answer this question with a 'yes'.

A film worth seeing, the American thriller *The Game* (1997) with Michael Douglas, about the practices of the Church of Scientology, gives a complete picture for anyone interested.

A brief description of the threefold social order as an aid to understanding the following chapters

Rudolf Steiner demonstrated in numerous presentations that humanity is a threefold organism. This threefoldness is important in the further context of this book, so a summary of this theme is given below.

The life, operations and activity of humanity are divided into the following spheres: the sphere of thought, the sphere of law and the state, and the economic life.

In some form or another everyone participates in this division, but each in their individual way according to their nature and destiny.

These three divisions can only work together harmoniously when the laws appropriate to each are respected. These are: freedom in the sphere of thought, equality in legal matters, and brotherliness in commercial life.

We recognize in these ideas the slogans of the French Revolution: *Liberté, Égalité, Fraternité.*

What do they mean?

Intellectual and cultural life can only unfold when those who work in this area are allowed to develop their projects in *freedom.*

Who are the people working in the life of thought? Everyone who creates culture: teachers, artists, doctors, priests, judges, inventors, scientists.

Everyone has areas in their professional life where they can be creative if they are given the requisite freedom to be so.

Each of us also lives within the parameters of the law in which the principle of *equality* is applicable. Before the law we are all the same. This means the law constitutes a framework we must all observe. All road-users must drive on the right in countries where the law is to keep right, or on the left in counties where the law is to keep left.

The principle of *economic activity* is *brotherliness*. What is meant here is that in trade we have consideration for our trading-partner, because if things go badly for our partner, then they will eventually also go badly for those connected with them in economic activity. This attitude in life is a profoundly Christian one. We earlier discussed creation out of nothing, which happens when we do something positive out of our own will that we are not obliged to do. This attitude is 'balm' for economic life. It brings an impulse to situations in life that solves problems.

Humanity has always organized itself in this threefold order—into a sphere of thought, a sphere of the law, and a sphere of commerce—but often in an unbalanced way. Usually it was legalistic thinking that predominated, with a legalistic approach in the foreground that sought to solve problems by the application of rigid rules which were also applied in the intellectual and economic life.

Rudolf Steiner called a state operating in this way a *unitary state*. In the threefold social organism proposed by Steiner, each of the three sections would be autonomous. In this way they would *learn* how to function together harmoniously.

Steiner discussed and answered the many questions that naturally arise in connection with realizing the threefold social order, in his book *Die Kernpunkte der sozialen Frage in den Lebensnotwendigkeiten der Gegenwart und der Zukunft*[53] (Core issues of the social question for the requirements of life in the present and the future).

Why is the threefold impulse so important? Because it could free humanity from its spiritual and intellectual rigidity. For, by working on the threefolding idea, we learn to grasp developments in a new way when they are unable to progress further out of themselves.

The different nature of peoples in the West, in the Centre, and in the East, and the emergence of egoless individuals

Developing this theme further, the spiritual researcher shows that hatred and destructive intentions oppose the threefolding idea. In this context he speaks once more about egoless people.[54]

Rudolf Steiner discusses this as part of a description of the different nature of people in the West, in the Centre, and in the East:

> Everything in the spiritual and intellectual development of the new era is predisposed to promoting the individual—the individual in the West in the Western way, in a commercial way; the individual in the Centre in the now antiquated state-political-cal-military way; the individual in the East in the antiquated way of old spirituality, now completely decadent. This has to be carried by the spiritual world. And it is carried by the appearance in the West and in the East—we'll restrict ourselves to just these two areas for the moment—of a strange, profoundly significant phenomenon. It is that an unusually large number of people—at least a relatively large number—are being born who do not show the regular course of reincarnation [...] What we encounter as a human being in human form doesn't always have to be what it appears to be. The outer appearance can be just that: appearance. We can encounter people in human form who only in their outer appearance are individuals subject to repeated lives on earth; in truth, these are humans with a physical, etheric, and astral body, but beings are embodied in them, beings that make use of these individuals in order to operate through them. It is a fact that in the West for example, there is a large number of such people who are basically not straightforwardly reincarnated human beings but who are carriers of beings who show a decidedly premature course of evolution, who should actually only appear in human form at a later evolutionary stage.[55]

We'll pause the quotation for a moment and ask what it can mean that beings who appear within humanity 'in a premature course of evolution,' but are not human, make use of the human body? What kind of beings are they? And does their premature appearance in human form mean that, according to world karma, beings of this kind should intervene in evolution in later epochs, and that their activity already today is an abnormality?

And further: are they ahrimanic beings appearing in human form? And are they aware that they are not human?

From what Steiner goes on to say in this lecture, we can assume we are dealing here with ahrimanic beings. Prematurity corresponds to this kind of being. Steiner continues:

> Now, these beings do not make use of the whole human organism but primarily the metabolic system of these Western individuals. Of the three systems of human nature they utilize the metabolic system in such a way that they work through these people into the physical world. It is evident, even externally, to someone who can observe life properly that this is the situation with these individuals. Thus, for example, a large number of people who are members of Anglo-Saxon secret societies—we have discussed the role of such secret societies on a number of occasions in past years—the members of these secret societies, which have a great deal of influence, are actually bearers of these premature existences that work into the world through the metabolic system of certain individuals, and seek out a field of operation in the bodies of humans who do not live in regular reincarnations. Likewise the leading personalities of certain sects, and particularly the majority of a very widespread sect with a large following in the West, consist of individuals of this kind. In this way, I should like to put it like this, a completely different kind of spirituality works into present-day humanity. And it will be an important task to be able to approach life from these perspectives.[56]

These beings use human bodies in order to achieve something that deviates from normal evolution. Rudolf Steiner makes us aware that today (the today of 1920 can be extended to the today of the beginning of the twenty-first century and beyond, for the issue of egoless people has certainly increased since then) we would have to diagnose large areas of humanity in their daily intentions as foreign bodies for development as a whole. But this is not only about the larger masses where one might tend to assume the presence of egolessness, but about the leaders of secret societies and sects. This means that these groups are dominated by a non-human species of being intent on implementing non-human objectives.

What is *human*? A species of being that can have understanding for human beings and their bodily, soul-psychological, and intellectual-spiritual needs. Ultimately this is a question of how a human being can develop in soul and spirit. We understand this to be the actual Christian element. But these beings wish to shut this off from people's understanding and sensibilities.

Turning once more to the text of the lecture, we read that in the West there are in total three kinds of being that assert themselves and utilize human bodies. We have already mentioned the *first kind*, concerning which Steiner continues:

> The first kind are spirits that have a particular attraction to what in a sense are the elemental forces of the earth, [...] they can therefore have a sense for how colonization can be carried out in a particular place according to the natural conditions of climate and other conditions of the earth, or how to set up trading connections there and so on.[57]

The *second kind* works particularly in the rhythmic system. Rudolf Steiner does not state this expressly, but it follows from the context. They suppress the consciousness-soul of other people so that these people develop a kind of addict's disregard for the true motives for their actions. This leads to superficiality, empty formulaic words, and mendacity.

The *third kind* of being uses the nerve-sense system of the human body in which it is incarnated. They work in such a way that other people forget the individual capacities they bring with them out of the spiritual world and from previous lives. Through the influence of these beings that walk around in human bodies, they become like stereotype clichés of their race and nationality. These spirits see it as their task to prevent human beings from coming to their individual spirituality.

Through their particular nature, the effect all three groups have on other people is such that followers and pupils are recruited in epidemic proportions. As mentioned above, these spirits are to be found in leading positions in secret societies and sects.

What do they hope to achieve?

> Their objective is to maintain the whole of life as a mere economic life, to gradually eradicate everything else that is part of the intellectual and spiritual life, to eradicate the spiritual life precisely where it is most active, where it is shrunk into the abstraction of Puritanism, to gradually debilitate the life of politics and the state, and swallow up everything through the economic life. In the West it is these people, who work in the world in this way, who are the actual enemies and opponents of the threefold impulse.[58]

In this description of the three groups of beings, Rudolf Steiner draws attention to the pathological influences that threaten the social organism from the West. It is precisely the West which, from a spiritual-historical perspective, has the task of developing economic life or, put more exactly, of cultivating a mode of thought that grasps the importance of economics and puts its knowledge to practical use.

What more is meant when Steiner says that the people of the West have the task of developing an economic mode of thinking? What is meant initially is that through this mode of thought the forces of the consciousness-soul can be developed. They are developed when we train ourselves to learn from daily life. Through this we establish a basic objective attitude towards the facts of daily life which can prompt us to contain and hold in balance the tendencies in our wish-nature that incline towards excess. Also connected with the economic mode of thinking is a development and strengthening of the forces of will. Being an entrepreneur means having the ability to realize plans and adapt to circumstances in the process. Willpower is always also Ego-power, which can develop in this way. The egoless individuals we are describing also have an Ego-power that works with intense effect, but is not human. This can be seen in the fact that these individuals cannot learn from facts. They want to realize their programme or ideology by sticking rigidly to an agenda. There is no development of the consciousness-soul in these individuals. That they are enemies of the threefold idea is clear from what has been said above. In order to reach a brotherly attitude in economic life such as is required by the idea of a social three-foldness, a person working in this way would have to develop their consciousness-soul even more strongly than is otherwise required in life. They would also have to develop a mindset in their economic activity that looks beyond their own egotistical advantage, and that takes into account in a positive way in their thinking and dealings the economic situation of their trading-partner or partners. This again would be something profoundly Christian which the West has not developed up to now.

The contrary is the case. The West's market-economy ideology is spread over all humanity, exposing it to a ruthless mindset of competition. It follows from this that egoless individuals in the West are at the helm, and impress their ideology with suggestive power into cultural civilization. The willingness of present leaders to learn is slight, and it will take enormous catastrophes—particularly economic ones—before a spiritual and new orientation can be established.

Was the Lehman Brothers global financial crash in New York in the autumn of 2008 just a gentle foretaste of the catastrophes that await us?

In the same lecture, Steiner turns his gaze to the East: 'The East once had a sublime spiritual life. All spirituality, with the exception of what is aspired to in anthroposophy and wishes to take on new form, all the spirituality of the civilized world is basically an heirloom from the East.'[59]

But this inheritance is also a hindrance for the people of the East. It has not remained at its spiritual height but has become decadent. The effect of this inheritance is that the Eastern individual can easily enter into mediumistic states whereby beings in the East can then assert themselves by influencing these individuals in their sleep. Due to being more loosely incarnated, Eastern people—Asians and Russians—easily become the recipients of inspirations. These emanate from beings which, unlike in the West, do not incarnate in human bodies but influence Eastern people in their sleep. It is again three groups of spirits who are also opponents of the threefold social order.

The *first type* operates in a way that prevents people from penetrating and taking full possession of their physical body. Because of this the individual does not connect with the economic life or with what is going on in public life around them.

These spirits want to prevent a well functioning and well organized economic life from developing in the East.

The *second type* of being influences the individual so that they develop an *unegoistical egotism*. These individuals 'want to be completely good, they want to be as good as anyone can be. This is also an egotistical feeling. This is something that can definitely be designated paradoxically as an unegotistic egotism, an egotism produced by an imagined selflessness.'[60] If we want to be good only so that we can have a pleasant life in our next incarnation, then this is a double egotism. One wants to be ethical in order to receive a reward in one's next life. This attitude destroys the sphere of law and rights.

Why? Because someone who from a spiritual perspective looks at how the law functions, also accepts that people of the most diverse abilities and circumstances must all be treated equally before the law, otherwise justice becomes injustice.

Thus the self-image of the 'unegotistical egotist' cannot exist before spiritual law, because he is demanding a separate existence for himself.

Through the *third type* of spirit the spiritual life is suffocated by a vague mystical atmosphere. Sultry mysticism is a phenomenon at home mainly in the East and is frequently described by poets. Suffocation in a mysticism of this kind is brilliantly portrayed in psychological terms by Andrei Bely (1860-1934) in his novel *The Silver Dove*.[61]

The spirits of the East are referred to as 'beings of arrested development' who went through their stage of perfection in former times but today have become retrogressive. They are luciferic beings.

Rudolf Steiner describes these spirits of the West and East principally in connection with the threefold social order and its realization. He brings to his audience's attention the hostility towards the threefold social order coming from the supersensory level. In terms of our subject we can view his statements as a key to diagnosing the present situation of humanity. For here egoless individuals play a particular part.

Before going further, let us look at the people of the Centre. They too are endangered, but now from embodiments of beings of both the West and the East.

When they are *awake*, the people of the Centre are exposed to attacks by the spirits of the West whose effect works on their urges and instincts and paralyses their will. When they are *asleep*, the spirits of the East seek to influence them. On the whole, however, people of the Centre are less susceptible to the influences we have described. But they do exist.

Rudolf Steiner's statements call upon us to become diagnosticians of the events of our present times.

Our question now is how, by what means, can egoless individuals be recognized? Are there examples?

One example that is strikingly unambiguous is that of Adolf Hitler. He had a suggestive influence on his environment, indeed even unleashing a psychological epidemic in

the German people. The crowds were enraptured by his presence and his speeches. He created a fanatical following who
were not able to form their own judgement concerning
Hitler's nature and goals.

These adherents were willing assistants in his gruesome,
evil orders. The Hungarian-British journalist, Gitta Sereny, who
wrote a book about Hitler's architect and minister for armaments
and war production, Albert Speer, writes the following about her
conversations with Speer:

> In our conversations there were two themes I wanted to focus
> on. One was the origin of the evil in Hitler [which in my opin-
> ion went beyond his compulsive hatred of Jews and his crimes
> against them—E.G.], and the other was Speer's knowledge of this
> evil in Hitler and Speer's participation in the crimes that ema-
> nated from it. To some extent Hitler's genius lay in his ability to
> pervert others.[62]

With this ability Hitler perverted the whole German nation,
many valuable individualities—including Albert Speer. Gitta
Sereny writes that Speer did not become immoral or amoral, 'but
had become something far worse—*a morally extinguished human
being'.*[63]

So as to have as many aspects as possible, we will turn at
this point to a short account concerning egoless people. Eliza
von Moltke (1859-1932) experienced the following with Rudolf
Steiner:

> At another time they [Rudolf Steiner and Eliza von Moltke] were
> walking along the street together when they saw someone they
> knew drive past, and Rudolf Steiner is supposed to have said,
> 'That man has barely enough Ego-strength left to complete this
> life, let alone for a new incarnation.' With that remark was indi-
> cated that at the present time there is such a thing as an extin-
> guishing of Egos.[64]

How can an egoless person be recognized? Among other things they are distinguishable by having no *destiny motif*. They are karma-less strangers whose foreignness is not immediately apparent because they adapt straightaway to those around them. They are easily hurt when feeling excluded, and infinitely grateful for people's concern and affection.

What is a destiny motif?

The most unique characteristic of a person is what they have brought with them as spiritual harvest from previous lives, and what they aspire to in this life. We can observe this unique characteristic already in children. It is to be distinguished from behaviours that arise through heredity, which are not of equal status with characteristics that develop through imitation. For it is precisely in imitation that the individuality shimmers through, since the child does not imitate everything it experiences but rather chooses, from all the imitation-possibilities on offer, an individual selection. Rudolf Steiner describes this process:

> Imagine, let's say, a rash short-tempered father in the child's environment, who does all sorts of things that are actually not good. Because the child is all sense-organ it is obliged to absorb all these things just as the eye cannot defend itself against what it has to see, against what is in its surroundings. But it is only while the child is awake that it takes in what it perceives here. Then the child goes to sleep. Children sleep a great deal. And while it is sleeping, the child makes the selection. What it wants to absorb it sends down from its soul into its body. What it doesn't want to absorb it expels during sleep into the etheric world, so that the child only takes into its bodily nature what it is predetermined to take according to its destiny through its karma, through its destiny. We see the reigning power of destiny particularly vividly in the very first years of childhood.[65]

It is a matter of recognizing already in childhood the individuality in the revelation of its being. And it is from this revelation of being that the destiny motifs take shape. Egoless individuals do not have destiny motifs since these emanate from the Ego.

We get a clear picture of what a destiny motif is in the life of Goethe. He writes in *Dichtung und Wahrheit* (Poetry and Truth) how, as a six- or seven-year-old boy he wanted to hold a devotional service by assembling things from nature and arranging them on a four-sided music stand used for quartets.

> The boy could not give this being [God] a form; he therefore sought him in his works and wanted to set up an altar to him in good Old-Testament fashion. Things from nature would be used as a simile to represent the world, and above this a flame would burn signifying the human heart yearning for its creator. The best representative levels and examples were chosen from a collection of natural objects that had been gathered and was available; but the question was how to arrange and order the things. His father had a fine red-lacquered music stand with gold flowers, in the shape of a four-sided pyramid with various levels, that was very good for quartets although it had not been used much recently. The boy requisitioned this and now built up his representatives of nature at different levels one above the other, so that it looked very cheerful and yet sufficiently significant at the same time. The first devotions were to be carried out early at sunrise; but the young priest could not decide how to get a flame that would also emit a fragrance. At last he got an idea of how to achieve both. He had some {small, cone-shaped} incense sticks which, although they did not flame, did glow and gave off the most pleasant smell. Indeed, this softer burning and smoking seemed to express more clearly than an open flame what is happening in the human breast. The sun had been up for some time, but the East was blocked by neighbouring houses. At last it appeared above the roof-tops. Immediately a magnifying-glass was taken up and the incense cone, at the pinnacle in a beautiful porcelain bowl, was lit. Everything went as had been hoped for, and the devotions were completed. The altar remained as a special adornment of the room in which it had been given a place in the new house. Everyone saw it just as a nicely arranged nature collection. The boy knew better, but kept silent. He longed to repeat the ceremony. Unfortunately, when the most suitable sunrise occurred, the porcelain cup was not to hand; he put the incense cone directly on the surface of the top of the music stand; it was lit, and his devotions were so strong

that the priest did not notice the damage his oblation was doing until it was too late. The cone had burnt a shameful hole in the red lacquer and the lovely gold flowers, as though an evil spirit had disappeared and left its indelible black footprint behind.[66]

What is happening here is both a manifestation of the nature of Goethe's individuality and of the fundamental element that would later become a motif in his life: to find in transient things a simile for what is enduring, for what is eternal.

Even as a boy Goethe demonstrated this quality of turning his mind to what was living as spirit in the phenomena of nature. And what was living in Goethe was a life-motif he brought with him from previous lives. Rudolf Steiner points to this: 'We see here— since this characteristic, if we can put it like this, must have emanated from an original predisposition, could not have come from his environment—how what he brought with him into this incarnation worked particularly strongly in this individual.'[67]

We can look at a second example of a life-motif that also showed itself in childhood: a karmic situation in the life of the philosopher Johann Gottlieb Fichte (1762-1814). As a child he lived in village surroundings. His father was a ribbon weaver. He gave the boy his first lessons in reading and writing.

The philosopher's son, Immanuel Hermann Fichte (1796-1879), who also later became a philosopher, relates the following:

> Around the age of seven the boy was given a book by his father. It was the saga of *Horn-clad Siegfried* and completely captivated him. He read it over and over again and neglected his daily tasks as a result. He lost interest in everything else. He became aware that the cause of this loss of interest was his beloved book. He decided to separate himself from it and threw it, not without a struggle to master himself, into the village stream. The loss cost him many tears. When his father found him crying, the boy was unable to explain to his father what had happened, and Johann Gottlieb was severely punished for destroying the valuable book.[68]

What is the motif of destiny and character that comes to expression in this event?

It is the impulse of self-training. The boy Fichte brings a strong Ego into this incarnation that already in childhood directs his actions, is also able to check his wish-nature, and determine his action through a goal set by his Ego.

How did Fichte affect his contemporaries?

> One could call Fichte a 'worldview enthusiast'. With this enthusi-asm he must have had an entrancing effect on his contemporaries and students. Let us hear what one of these latter, Forberg, says of him: 'His public lecture sweeps along like a thunder storm that releases its fire in separate strikes [...]; he lifts the soul.' He does not wish to make just good people, but great people. His eye is censorious and his gait defiant [...], he wishes with his philosophy to direct the spirit of the age [...]. His imagination is not flowery but energetic and powerful [...]. The most striking characteristic of Fichte's personality is the great, serious style of his view of life.[69]

We will close this brief look at Fichte with the following question: What is the goal of human evolution? With Fichte in mind we can say: Inner freedom which the human individual attains through his or her own effort, is the goal and meaning of our life. Fichte:

> A god could create me; but he would have to leave it up to me to recognize myself as an 'I'. I give myself my ego-consciousness. In this I do not have a realization, a recognition, that I have received, but one I have made myself.[70]

In these words Fichte sums up the motif of his life, which is at the same time a revelation of his nature. Despite its inner fire, his Ego-force has humility. It is expressed in the following sentence: 'There is nothing important in my person, but everything in the truth, for I am a priest of the truth.'[71]

This look at Ficthe's nature and philosophy is based on what Steiner has written in his book *Die Rätsel der Philosophie* (Riddles of Philosophy).

Death by potassium cyanide and its effect on the Ego

We turn now to a subject which during the period of National Socialism became a horrendous fact: death by potassium cyanide. Through their military operations in Eastern Europe, the National Socialists aimed to create space for German settlements. There were also many Jews living in these regions. Together with the 'Slavic sub-humans' (Nazi terminology), they were brutally driven out and murdered.

The systematic murder of Jews was decided upon as the 'final solution of the Jewish question' at the Wannsee conference on 20 January 1942 in the Berlin SS guesthouse (on the Wannsee). The killing was carried out predominantly with *potassium cyanide*. What this means is elucidated in the following.

On 10 October 1923 Steiner gave a lecture to the workers engaged in the building of the Goetheanum, in which he discusses in detail 'the question of potassium cyanide'.

> But now, in the way we are today on the earth, if we introduce potassium cyanide into ourselves, it destroys all the movements and life-forces in our body. But the bad thing is that, when someone poisons themselves with potassium cyanide, there is always the danger that it takes the soul with it and the person, instead of being able to live on in soul, is dispersed into the whole cosmos, and specifically dispersed in sunlight.[72]

We will let these sentences sink in and emphasize inwardly that the spiritual teacher says that cyanide poisoning does not only destroy the physical body but can annihilate *the soul and spirit* as well. But we note that Rudolf Steiner did not formulate this in absolute terms but says that 'there is the danger' that soul and spirit are also annihilated. Thus it can also be possible that an individual can lose their life through cyanide poisoning but their soul and spirit are *not in every case* destroyed along with it, and it seems that further incarnations of this individual are possible.

If anthroposophical knowledge were widespread, no one would poison themselves with cyanide. It would never even enter their head! The fact that cyanide poisonings do occur is only a result of a materialistic worldview, because people think that death is death, and it's all the same whether one suffers death through cyanide or through an inner dissolution. But it is not all the same! When we die due to an inner dissolution, soul and spirit have the usual path to enter the spiritual world; they live on. But when someone poisons themselves with potassium cyanide, the soul has the intention to accompany every little particle of the body everywhere, and particularly to spread itself out in nitrogen and dissolve into the universe. This is the real death of the soul and spirit. If people knew that soul and spirit are the real human being, they would say: We couldn't possibly cause this terrible explosion which is brought about in a subtle way in the whole universe when a person poisons themself with cyanide. For every individual who poisons themself with cyanide intervenes in a wrong way in the stream that goes from the earth to the sun. And every time someone poisoned themself with cyanide we would see, if we had the appropriate instruments, a small explosion in the sun. And the sun becomes worse through it. The human being taints the universe and also the force that streams from the sun to the earth, when he poisons himself with potassium cyanide. The human being really has an influence on the universe. When someone poisons themself with cyanide, the fact is that they are actually ruining the sun! This is how it is with every cyanide poisoning.[73]

So what happens in a cyanide poisoning? The Ego is 'atomized' into countless tiny particles and dissolves in the universe. 'This is the real death of the soul and spirit,' according to Rudolf Steiner. It seems that continued existence after cyanide poisoning is not always possible. We will return to this question later on.

We are dealing here with the destruction of the Ego which Sorat—the horned beast of the Apocalypse—aspires to. He is the sun demon who opposes the rightful regent of the sun forces, Christ. The imbuing of humanity and the universe with Christian forces emanates from Christ.

Murdering Jews with cyanide is only one means by which Sorat and his human accomplices carry out evil.

Why did the spiritual researcher speak in October 1923 to the Goetheanum builders about the deadly effect of potassium cyanide? Did he foresee already in October 1923 the destruction of the Jews, which began with particular violence and cruelty at the same time as the German campaign against Russia in the summer of 1941? This could be. There are enough witnesses to Steiner's prescience to assume the possibility here.

But why did Steiner speak on this subject at all—and why to the workers at the Goetheanum, who for the most part were not anthroposophists but always listened to his lectures with the greatest of interest?

Steiner speaks about things in these lectures for the workers that were completely new to his audience. Presentations of this kind—particularly by a spiritual researcher—have an occult effect: they wake people up.

They are particularly effective when they lead to a question in the listener which can open the way for the spiritual researcher to say more. Even where this is not the case, what he says nevertheless has an awakening effect and is a helpful impulse in the individual's further development.

The reason why Rudolf Steiner spoke to the workers may also be that these individuals could receive what he had to say with less prejudice than overly intellectual people.

What does a person experience who crosses the threshold of death in the normal way? They see the life just lived passing before them backwards in etheric pictures. It is a tremendous sight in which the deceased person experiences themselves in their actions and thus is led to self-knowledge. The etheric body then dissolves into the cosmic ether with the exception of that part of the etheric body which the individual was able to spiritualize and purify during life. This portion remains with the individual as a force of their own being.

The astral body also dissolves, although over the much longer period of a third of the past life. Here too the Ego apprehends itself once more: the individual relives all the events and situations of their life, but experiences now what effect their actions and their whole nature had on others and on their surroundings.

The Ego learns by this. Our further existence after death in soul and spirit thus has an enormous significance for the Ego's evolution. It experiences who it is and what it could do in a future life to change bad into good and how this sequence of lives can proceed. It is told this by its angel.

All this appears to be no longer possible when the Ego has died by cyanide. What concerns us in a death by cyanide is the finality the human individual faces who has died in this way.

Is there no solution or liberation in this situation that would nevertheless enable further development to take place? We will gradually piece together a possible answer. So, to begin with, an account of a dream dreamt by Ernst Lehrs, himself of Jewish extraction.

A dream described by Ernst Lehrs

Ernst Lehrs (1894-1979) was a teacher at the first Waldorf school in Stuttgart. He taught upper school sciences. In his autobiography *Gelebte Erwartung* (Experienced expectation)[74] he relates a dream he had about his mother who was murdered by the National Socialists.

> Because of its content which is more than just personal to me, I will here mention a dream that granted me a message from the world in which my mother's soul found itself after death [...]. It happened shortly after her memorial service, mentioned earlier. {In the dream} I found myself at the edge of a forest standing at a barrier made of logs. In the distance I could make out a clearing in which there was movement of many human figures. A female doctor whom I had known formerly and who had died a number of years previously, approached {from the clearing} and came up to the barrier. She bowed slightly towards me and gave me a message with the following content: Caroline von Heydebrand—who, along with the connection to Maria Röschl and myself as a colleague, was also a close friend of us both—wanted me to know that over there a continuous healing cultus was taking place for the souls who were violently expelled from life by the events on earth, in which she herself was performing a priestly function, and had the soul of my mother ministering at her side.[75]

Can dreams have messages from the dead for the living? This question can be answered with a yes. And the dream related by Ernst Lehrs is a clear example of how a 'conversation' can take place between the living and the deceased. However, the living person must cultivate a particular mood if the deceased one is to reach them. This mood arises through the following exercise: In the course of life we reach crossing-points that leave open a number of possibilities for our continued destiny.

An example: We are offered a job. If we accept the offer, life takes a certain direction with new tasks and perhaps important new people.

> When anthroposophy awakens a feeling in people for the {many} possibilities {that could happen} in life, for certain events and shocks that did not occur for the simple reason that something {else} for which the forces were present did not take place—when this is felt, and the soul holds fast to a feeling of this nature, then the soul is indeed suited to receive experiences from the spiritual world from persons with whom it had a connection in the physical world. Although during the turbulence of daily life people are for the most part unsuited to giving themselves up to feelings about what might have happened, there are nevertheless times in life in which this 'what might have happened' has a definite effect on the soul. If you were to observe more closely the life of dreams or the strange life of transition from waking to sleeping or from sleeping to waking, if you were to look more closely at certain dreams which are sometimes completely inexplicable, where something or other that is happening to us comes before our soul in a dream-picture or a vision—if the soul were to pursue this, it would find that these inexplicable pictures are something that could have happened and was only prevented from doing so because other conditions intervened than those that could have happened, or because other obstacles somehow intervened. Someone who through meditation or some other method develops mobility in their thinking, will have moments in waking life in which they feel—albeit not as a clear definite mental picture but just as a feeling—how they are living in a world of potentialities. When we develop a feeling such as this, we prepare ourselves to receive impressions from the spiritual world from those with whom we were connected in the physical world. And then influences like this come to light in such moments as we have just described, as dream experiences, but which have genuine significance, which refer to something real in the spiritual world.[76]

What is it that Ernst Lehr's late mother wishes to communicate to him from the spiritual world? She wants to tell him that she is participating in a healing cultus that gives helping forces to those who have been killed, so that the total annihilation of the Ego by cyanide is revoked. We can at least allow ourselves this interpretation, even if these were not the actual words verbatim.

A conversation with Rudolf Steiner about potassium cyanide

We get a more satisfactory answer to the question as to whether people who have died by cyanide poisoning can be 'saved', from the doctor Georg Groot (1899-1967). He relates a conversation he was able to have with Rudolf Steiner when, as a young man, Groot was doing guard duty at the Goetheanum.[77]

> From the Goetheanum fire on New Year's Eve 1922 until October 1928, I performed watch duty at the Goetheanum. During this time I had the opportunity to have a number of conversations with Rudolf Steiner. One of these conversations took place on 13 October 1923. I had spent the night on guard duty in house 'Hansi' where Rudolf Steiner lived, and it was also my job to guard Rudolf Steiner's walk from villa 'Hansi' to the Schreinerei (carpentry studio). Rudolf Steiner spoke to me as he left the house, and I used the opportunity to ask him what for me was a very burning question. A few days earlier I had had the opportunity to listen behind a wall in the Schreinerei to a lecture given by Steiner to the workers. In this lecture Steiner said that in a case of cyanide poisoning [*Blausäurevergiftung*] the human soul was destroyed, and could not enter the sun sphere by the straight path, but only by many detours. Because I could not imagine how a physical substance of material origin could have a continued influence on the soul after death, I put this question to Rudolf Steiner. He was immediately willing to explain. He said roughly the following: 'The human etheric body is bound to the physical body by oxygen. The moment cyanide enters the body, oxygen is converted to nitrogen. This tears the etheric body to shreds, so the person also has no {panoramic} review. The hierarchies still have an interest in saving the human soul, which is awful work for them.'
>
> To my question as to whether cyanide gas would be used in the next war, he answered in the negative, but said other terrible

things were being prepared. To my question whether this would happen in America, he said, 'No, in Germany!' Later in the conversation Rudolf Steiner came to speak of the permeating of the etheric world with Christian forces, and said that then people would be inclined to accept spiritual teachings. He also indicated that one would have to forbid the construction of ahrimanic machines. Just as today it is regarded as immoral to gun someone down just because we don't like them, so moral laws would also have to be applied to ahrimanic machines. When he asked if I understood what he meant, I said, 'Yes.' This was a great shortcoming on my part, believing I knew everything, and so didn't ask the necessary question. That not all machines were meant by this became clear to me later. Rudolf Steiner surely had something specific in mind. With this problem the conversation was in all essentials concluded.

In another conversation which took place before the Christmas Conference of 1923, I asked Rudolf Steiner how one could do one's spiritual work in a way that enabled one to turn consciously to one's angel. As a prelude to this question, I should mention that some time before this conversation I mentioned to Steiner my wish to become a doctor and asked if he thought this would be right. He was pleased and approved, but advised me against studying medicine at a university. He said he would help me along personally himself, and gave me some instructions. I was given permission to attend the medical course, and also the pastoral medical course. [...] Returning to my question, Rudolf Steiner gave me the following guidance which, with his express permission, I could pass on to my friends. Rudolf Steiner said roughly the following: 'If you want to investigate, for example, the relationship between the liver and spleen, study on one day everything you can find on the liver in my books. After three and a half days you must have forgotten everything. After another three and a half days—so after seven days—study everything about the spleen. After another three and a half days you must have forgotten everything. After these three and a half days fourteen days will have passed.* Because the human is a limited being, you must wait another seven days—so 21 days in all counting from the first day. Then you'll have it! You can do the same with months and years, but not with weeks.'

I include this indication from Rudolf Steiner in my account concerning cyanide poisoning, because many of my colleagues will be able to make something of it. The fact that I then went and studied at a university anyway was the second great mistake in this incarnation. But it is all part of one's personal development.[78]

If we allow these words of Rudolf Steiner's to resonate in us, it becomes clear that death by cyanide is not only an earthly event but something that concerns the hierarchies as well. They want to rescue the human soul. But this is 'awful work' for them. The higher spirit-beings nevertheless want to help the individuals in question to shoulder their future incarnation which has been so impeded. The tone of Steiner's words, however, are such as to make us think the forces the hierarchies can pour into human evolution are not unlimited.

We might imagine that a person would be reborn with handicaps as though as a punishment for the cyanide death. But the opposite is the case. In such a situation destiny promotes development with special forces so that the balance of forces is compensated, and someone who has suffered this terrible death is reborn with particularly strong forces.

We also emphasize the following from Georg Groot's account: namely, that Rudolf Steiner said people must be stopped from constructing ahrimanic machines.

---

* Translator's footnote: There seems to be some mistake here, since 3 x 3½ days = 10½ days, not 14 days. Perhaps this last sentence should read 'After *another* three and a half days fourteen days will have passed.'

What kind of machines could these be? In our view they are computers or computer-like machines that result in computer addiction and mislead people into regarding what happens on a screen as actual reality. This attitude weakens the Ego. The Ego is overrun by the events appearing on the screen. The force at work here can be seen, as an Imagination, as locusts stripping everything bare.

Thinking further on this question, we can assume that the spiritual world—its beings and also non-incarnated human souls—works to overcome and to heal the evil done to people killed by cyanide.

A special quality Georg Groot had should also still be mentioned: he could heal by the laying on of hands. However, this ability grew less during the course of his life.[79]

The human Ego and spiritual economy
in its development

In this book we have attempted to comprehend the manifold mysteries of the Ego.

Together with the particular issue of egoless individuals, to which we will return later, we turn now to a further enigma of Ego-development, discussed by the spiritual researcher as the idea of *spiritual economy*.[80]

What is spiritual economy? We can understand this concept when we make clear for ourselves what the goal of human evolution is. The task of human beings is to develop individually in soul and spirit.

Rudolf Steiner says in these stupendous lectures, that the human being is also a part of the hierarchies, but is able to make his contribution to the whole of evolution out of his own will and freedom:

> When he looks to his future, he can say: I am called upon to look in my deepest inner being for everything that gives me the impulse to act—not by beholding the Godhead, like the Seraphim, but out of my deepest inner being. And Christ is a god whose working is not such that it must be followed unconditionally, but only when we agree with and understand it, only in freedom...[81]

In every life on earth we are given the opportunity by spiritual guidance to take further strides in our development.

We are helped in this by the spiritual world and its beings. Apart from the angels—the angeloi, archangeloi, and archai— there are other helpers: masters, bodhisattvas, and avatars.

Rudolf Steiner also refers to the masters as 'the masters of wisdom and the harmony of feelings':

> This individual [a master, E.G.] is one who has been through many incarnations and, through meditation, through a pious life, has attained something different from other people, so that the

individual has run ahead of humanity and attained forces which the rest of humanity will only attain in the future.[82]

There are twelve masters who guide humanity as the 'Great Lodge' or the 'White Lodge'. In the midst of these masters, as the thirteenth, is Christ who fills the masters with his spiritual power. This circle of masters is permeated by the twelve bodhisattvas, who also give impulses for the guidance and evolution of humanity. Bodhisattvas are human beings who are so highly evolved that they are ensouled by an archangel as far as their etheric body.

In the following we will discuss the problem of spiritual economy. In order to understand this we need to realize that spiritual beings can mutually interpenetrate one another. People also penetrate other people consciously or unconsciously, living and deceased, or accommodate higher beings in the structure of their members-of-being.

We can look at the nature of an *avatar*. What is an avatar? An avatar is a person, or better to say a being who appears in human form to help humanity and give it spiritual impulses. An avatar is not seeking anything for itself by its help and incarnations, because it has already reached the goal of evolution and is now able to bestow its forces on humanity. The greatest avatar is Christ. He is the Sun-being who, through the Baptism by John, fully permeated the human Jesus.

> Christ is the greatest avatar who descended to earth; and when a being of such nature descends into earthly existence as Christ was in Jesus, something mysterious, something of the highest significance occurs. Just as when, on a smaller scale, we plant a grain of wheat in the earth, it germinates and a stalk grows from it, and ears of corn which bear many, many grains that are replicas of the single wheat grain we laid in the ground, so it is also with the spiritual world. For 'all transient things are but a simile'* —and in this proliferation of the grain of wheat we see an image, a simile, of the spiritual worlds.

---

* Quote from Goethe: *'alles Vergängliche ist nur ein Gleichnis'*- P.K.

When the event of Golgotha took place, something happened to the etheric body and astral body of Jesus of Nazareth: through the power of the indwelling Christ they [the etheric body and astral body—E.G.] were multiplied, and since then many, many replicas of the astral body and etheric body of Jesus of Nazareth have existed in the spiritual world. And these replicas continued to be active.

When a human individuality descends from spiritual heights to earthly existence, it clothes itself in an etheric body and an astral body. But when there is something in the spiritual worlds such as replicas of the etheric body and astral body of Jesus of Nazareth, then for someone in whose karma such a thing lies, something very special happens. After the Mystery of Golgotha, when an individual's karma allowed, a replica of the etheric body or astral body of Jesus of Nazareth was woven into them. This was the case with Augustine (354-430), for example, in the first centuries of our calendar. As this individuality descended from spiritual heights and clothed itself in an etheric body, a replica was woven into this etheric body of the etheric body of Jesus of Nazareth. The individuality had its own astral body and Ego, but had woven into its etheric body a replica of the etheric body of Jesus of Nazareth.

Thus what had enveloped the god-human-being of Palestine was transferred to other human beings who were now to carry the quality of this great impulse into the rest of humanity. Because Augustine was reliant on his own Ego and his own astral body, he was exposed to all the doubts, waverings, and errors which were hard for him to overcome; they emanated from these still-imperfect parts of his being. Everything he went through he went through due to his erroneous judgement and the errors of his Ego. But once he had fully permeated himself, once his etheric body began to take effect, he came upon the forces that were woven into him from the replica of the etheric body of Jesus of Nazareth in his own etheric body. And then he became one who was able to preach to the Occident a part of the great truths of the mysteries.[83]

Many Christian painters of the Middle Ages had just such a replica of the etheric body of Jesus of Nazareth woven into them. These were wonderful pictures of the events of Christianity, behind which were Imaginations experienced by the painters. And this painting tradition derives from the immanence of replicas of the etheric and astral body of Jesus.

> What we have as pictures depicting the event of Golgotha derives from people in whom were woven such replicas of the etheric body of Jesus. Precisely because of this they saw in their visions the event of Golgotha and what was connected with it. [...] When Christ was embodied in Jesus of Nazareth, something like an imprint of Christ's 'I' was created in the astral body of Jesus of Nazareth. [...] This replica of the 'I' of Christ in the body of Jesus produced numerous copies which were preserved, so to speak, in the spiritual world.[84]

So these replicas have arisen through the Mystery of Golgotha— replicas of the etheric body, astral body, and also the Ego. The replicas are multiplied in the spiritual world and 'preserved', and woven into many individuals over the course of time. However, individuals must make themselves sufficiently mature to receive a replica of the 'I' of Christ.

> It is part of the inner mission of the spiritual cosmic stream [anthroposophy, E.G.], to prepare people to attain a maturity of soul to the extent that now an ever increasing number of people can receive into themselves a copy of the Ego-being of Christ Jesus. For, the course of Christian development has been this: first, a widening propagation on the physical plane, then propagation through etheric bodies, then through astral bodies which were frequently the reincarnated astral bodies of Jesus. Now a time is to come when the I-nature of Christ Jesus himself emerges more and more in people as the innermost being of their soul.[85]

What constitutes spiritual economy? The following consideration can lead us to an answer: When an ordinary person dies, they experience that their etheric body dissolves and separates from them, except for the portion they were able to purify during the course of their life.

When an initiate dies, however, this process does not take place. He brings a purified and spiritualized etheric and astral body into the spiritual world, which does not dissolve but becomes a source of helping impulses for the living.

These purified and holy members-of-being are woven into suitable individuals.

Thus Francis of Assisi (1182-1226) had inwoven in his astral body a replica of the astral body of Jesus of Nazareth. So too did Elizabeth of Thuringia (1207-1361). Meister Eckhart (1260-1328) and Johannes Tauler (1300-1361) received a copy of Jesus' Ego.

These individuals thus became Christ-bearers and helpers of the Christ impulse. In the following, Rudolf Steiner compares Augustine with Thomas Aquinas (1227-1274):

> If we compare Aquinas with Augustine, we see that, unlike Augustine, he was not entangled in error, and from childhood onwards knew no doubt or lack of faith, because discernment and conviction have their seat in the astral body and he had received the astral body of Christ woven into his own astral body. The implanting of a principle [member-of-being] into a human body can only take place when an external factor alters the natural course of things. So when Thomas was still a child, there was a lightning strike close to him which killed his little sister. This physical, only apparently physical, event put him into a condition to receive the astral body of Christ into his own astral body.[86]

This occurrence is described by Karl Werner in his comprehensive biography of Thomas Aquinas, in the following words: 'Before his birth a pious hermit had foretold to his mother the future renown of her son; [...] in his youngest childhood he remained unharmed when a bolt of lightning struck the room and killed his little sister next to him.'[87]

Rudolf Steiner goes further into the following law: in a change in the course of things the spiritual world works directly into the physical. This is why the spiritual researcher refers to the bolt of lightning as only an apparent physical event, which was however necessary in order to implant into Thomas the astral body of Christ, which Thomas thus received as a small child.[88]

When we consider the connection between Rudolf Steiner and Thomas Aquinas, we can understand how Steiner was able to unveil in such a comprehensive way the mysteries of Christianity.

But the mysteries of Christianity are also the mysteries of the Ego; for the Christ impulse also strengthens the Ego.

When we ask what the mysteries of the Ego consist of, the following thoughts might lead us to an answer: 'All avatars have redeemed humanity by power from above, by what they caused to ray down to the earth from spiritual heights. But Christ as avatar has redeemed humanity through that which he drew from the forces of humanity itself, and has shown us that the forces of redemption, the forces for conquering matter, can be found through the spirit in ourselves.'[89]

In other words, the physical body must be spiritualized by the Ego to such an extent that the Christ impulse can flow directly into the physical body. In this way matter is conquered by spirit. Help for the spiritual pupil in accomplishing this can be given by eurythmy. In eurythmy, through the movement and gesture of the arms, but also of the whole body, a harmonizing force is directed into the physical body. These movements correspond to the supersensory gestures that take place in our aura when we speak and when we listen to speech. They occur during the recitation of poetry. Rudolf Steiner also refers to them as 'visible speech'. Although eurythmy is primarily a performing art, it has a therapeutic application as eurythmy therapy.

When we watch eurythmy, we see something supersensory.

The task of the gods

We began this book by asking whether there are people who do not have an Ego. We had to answer this question in the affirmative: yes, there are such people. There is always a peculiarity in the life and activity of these individuals: their sheaths are 'occupied' by a non-human being. This might be an elemental being which, after the death of this 'person', dissolves into the etheric world. But it might also be an evil ahrimanic or luciferic demon that does evil gratuitously.

The task of the gods is to transform human suffering and adversity into good fortune. Suffering and adversity are necessary, however, for people to advance in their soul-spiritual development.

> But what here on earth meets with little enthusiasm in our souls, like the sentence: I will choose [in my life plan before birth—E.G.] a great misfortune in order to become more perfect, because otherwise I would remain imperfect with regard to what is in my past karma—this perspective which, as I said, finds little enthusiasm in earthly life, exists, exists as a fully justified perspective when we are in the life between death and a new birth. So we look for a volcanic eruption, we look for an earthquake, so that by way of misfortune we find a way to perfection.
>
> These two different ways of looking at life, the one from the spiritual world and the other from the physical world, are something we definitely have to espouse.[90]

The spiritual researcher now draws our attention to the fact that people can die in two kinds of disaster: in *natural* disasters and in *civilizational* disasters. When death occurs through these events, a trans-karmic power intervenes in personal destiny. It is not possible for the personal life to be lived out, and in one moment the individual brings the un-lived-out aspect of their etheric body, astral body, and their Ego-structure into the spiritual world.

What do the beings of the three hierarchies do when people ascend to them who bring earthly aspects into the spiritual world in this way? The task arising for these beings is to bring back into the cosmic order what is apparently bent on evil, what is apparently bent on opposing the cosmic order. The gods have to reckon with this situation in order to transform ahrimanic evil into a higher good.[91]

When people die due to disasters, the situation for the hierarchies is as follows:

There are unused-up causes [because karma could not be lived out— E.G.]. And what is there as unused causes can be taken by the gods and brought to the individual, and thus strengthen him with regard to his inner being for his next life on earth. So that in a sense the violent power of what had reigned as the cause in a previous incarnation, breaks out all the more strongly in the individual in the next incarnation. Whereas, if he had not met such a disaster, he might have come into the world with less valuable capacities, or with abilities in a completely different area than is the case when he is reborn, the individual appears as a different person to balance out karma. But he appears with particular qualities. For his astral body is condensed, as it were, because unused causes have been incorporated into it.[92]

When we look at *civilizational* disasters, we note that the people involved are karmically not strongly connected. They are herded together, as it were, by the ahrimanic being in order to meet a common demise.

Let us look at a *natural* disaster:

In a person who meets with a natural disaster, a sharpened memory is evoked of everything contained in their karma as cause. For when the human being steps through the threshold of death he is reminded of everything contained in his karma. An intensification of this, a distinct memory due to the natural disaster occurs in the soul of an individual who was killed because of it.

A train crash, on the other hand, any kind of civilizational disaster, evokes a forgetting of karma. But due to this forgetting of karma, the human being becomes strongly receptive to the impressions they have once more from the spiritual world after death. And the result is that such a person now asks themself: How do things stand with the unused-up karma in me?

And whereas, in the case of a natural disaster, it is particularly intellectual qualities that are condensed in an individual's astral body, in civilizational disasters it is will qualities that are condensed and strengthened. This is how karma works.[93]

[...] and our attention, which must otherwise be focused with understanding, with full understanding, on human karma, is diverted from human destiny to the destiny of the gods. For when we follow the horrors of war, the guilt of war, the monstrousness of war in connection with natural and elemental disasters in which people are killed, we see expressed the battle of the good gods with gods that are evil in two directions. We see beyond human life into the life of the gods, and see the gods' life against the background of human life. And we see it first and foremost not from a perspective of dry theory, but see it with heart and interest, we see this life of the gods in such a way that we can look at it now in its connection with what occurs in the individual karma of people on earth, because we see human destiny and divine destiny as interwoven.

But when we look at such things, the world behind human beings will have moved very close to us. For then something becomes evident to us that we can view only with the very greatest interest and engagement. Then it is evident how human destiny is embedded in the gods' destiny, how in a certain sense the gods thirst for what they are to undertake with human beings out of the course of their own battle. And by drawing closer to such ideas, we return with them once again to what was carried into the world in the ancient days of clairvoyance through the mysteries.[94]

Against whom do the gods battle? Against the 'lower' or ahrimanic gods, and against the 'upper' or luciferic gods.

The good gods operate from a position of balance. And the mystery pupil is led to the question: 'Why is there a sum of misfortune in the world?' So that the gods can transform it into good fortune!

For good fortune alone does not lead us into cosmic existence. It is only good fortune arising from misfortune in our passage through the sense-world that leads us into the depths of the world.[95]

Then there are certainly moments which must also occur for those who are not superficial, in which karma can press down heavily on one. But all these moments are balanced out once more by those in which karma gives us wings, so that we rise with our soul out of the earthly realm into the divine realm. And we must feel deeply in our inner being the connection between the world of gods with the world of human beings if we wish to speak of karma in the true sense of the word.

For what clothes us and surrounds us in an earthly life is what initially perishes on the path between death and a new birth. What remains, however, is that by which the gods—the beings of the higher hierarchies, that is—take us by the hand. And no one will be able to develop the right mood of soul with regard to knowledge of karma, who does not regard knowledge of karma as a helping hand from the side of the gods.

So, my dear friends, try to grasp knowledge of karma in a way that evokes this feeling in you: By approaching through this knowledge holy spiritual ground where something concerning karma can become clear to me, I must take hold of the hand of the gods.

Our sensibilities must become this real if we wish to push through to actual knowledge of the spiritual world—and this is what karma knowledge is.[96]

The Christ impulse

The task we set ourselves in this book was to present a concise picture of our time and of present-day humanity, while at the same time showing the connection between the physical-material level and the spiritual world and its forces and beings.

We can ask: Is there something that opposes the evil forces working into our lives?

Yes, it is the Christ impulse! What is the Christ impulse?

It is the spiritual energy that emanates from Christ. St John's Gospel calls it the WORD that lives as creative power in all things. Every person who receives and assimilates the *words of Christ* participates in their divine power irrespective of the language in which this happens.

We read the following words of Christ: 'Heaven and Earth will pass away, but my words will not pass away.'[97]

Rudolf Steiner elucidates these Christ words in the following way:

> Human beings will absorb the impulse of the Mystery of Golgotha for as long as the earth exists. Then there will come an intervening period between 'Earth' and 'Jupiter' [in occultism, *Jupiter* is the aeon following the Earth]. Such an intervening period always involves not just the single planet; everything around it also changes, passes over into chaos, goes through a pralaya. It is not only the earth itself that changes in a pralaya but also the heaven that is part of it. But what has been given to the earth in the word spoken by Christ, and was ignited by him in those who recognized him, and will endure in those who recognize him—this is the true essence of the earth's existence. And we gain a proper understanding from the truth of this saying which indicates for us the course of things in the cosmos, how the earth and its heavenly aspect, its heavenly aspect seen from an earthly perspective, is changed when the earth has reached its goal and heaven and earth

have passed away. But the words of Christ, which can be spoken concerning heaven and earth, will endure. When we understand the Gospels properly, we feel their innermost impulse, we feel not just the truth but also the power of the word that communicates itself to us as energy and helps us stand firmly on the ground of the earth, and helps us look beyond the world when we absorb with full understanding the word: 'Heaven and Earth shall pass away, but my words will not pass away.'[98]

The goal of human evolution

The following statements concerning the goal of human evolution were made by Rudolf Steiner in the lecture cycle *Geistige Hierarchien und ihre Widerspiegelung in der physischen Welt*[99] (Spiritual hierarchies and their reflection in the physical world). The human being is also a part of the hierarchies, but is able to make his contribution to the totality of evolution out of his own will in freedom:

> Looking towards the future [the human being] can say to himself: I am called upon to seek in my deepest inner being everything that gives me the impulse for my actions—not from beholding the Godhead, like the Seraphim, but from my own deepest inner being. And Christ is not a god whose impulses must be followed unconditionally, but only when we understand them, only in freedom [...] We see here also that world evolution does indeed not just repeat itself, but the new emerges. For, a humanity such as the human being experiences it has never existed before, not in the angels, not in the archangels, not in the archai. Human beings have a completely new mission to fulfil in the world, a mission we have just described. And it is for this mission that he has descended into the earthly world. And Christ has arisen for him in the world as a free helper, not as a god who operates from above, but as the first-born among many.
>
> And so we come to understand the full dignity and significance of human beings within the members of the hierarchies, and we say to ourselves as we look up to the glory and greatness of the higher hierarchies: Though they may be so great, so wise, so good that they could never stray from the right path, nevertheless it is the great mission of humankind to bring freedom into the world, and, with freedom, that which in the true sense of the word is called love. For without freedom, love is impossible.[100]

So the human being too belongs to the hierarchies. He represents the tenth stage. *He evolves by absorbing the Christ forces as a free deed.* When he has attained his goal, he will be the Spirit of Freedom or the Spirit of Love.

Conclusion:
Invisible spiritual beings
helping humanity develop spiritual science

In conclusion we will take a brief look at further findings presented by the spiritual researcher which show the sort of trials facing us in the future. These discussions are based on a lecture given by Steiner on 13 May 1921 at Dornach.[101]

Steiner draws our attention to the period spanning the withdrawal of the moon from the body of the earth—so before the Lemurian period—to the return of the moon in the eighth millennium. Modern science reckons with much longer time periods than those given by Steiner here. We will nevertheless base our discussion on Steiner's indications. Rudolf Steiner highlights that the gift of clairvoyance lasted into the fourth century after Christ. People were then guided mentally-spiritually by the intellect. In their intellect people became more and more shadowy, increasingly less able to truly grasp the real spiritual being of man with their thoughts. 'This shadowy intellect cannot understand the human being itself,' says the spiritual researcher.

Rudolf Steiner describes the situation before the withdrawal of the moon, when human beings sojourned in the planetary spheres and then returned after the withdrawal of the moon because conditions for life on earth were now conducive to their needs.

A significant event is described which occurred in the 70s and 80s of the nineteenth century:

> When in the ancient Atlantean period these human beings had returned from Saturn, Jupiter, Mars and so on, when human souls had taken on earthly existence, a time begins when other beings also descend from extraterrestrial cosmic regions, who are not human, but need to come to the earth for their further development, and to enter into a relationship with human beings on earth. Since the end of the 80s of the nineteenth century there have been extraterrestrial beings who want to enter earthly existence.

> Just as the Vulcan people were the last to come down to earth
> [in Atlantis], so there are Vulcan beings who are entering earthly
> existence now. We do indeed have extraterrestrial beings in
> earthly existence. And it is this circumstance that extraterrestrial
> beings are bringing down messages; it is thanks to this circum-
> stance that we can have a coherent spiritual science at all.[102]

Steiner is speaking about beings that are not human but who
need to descend to earth for their own development. But these
beings are not incarnated in a physical body. When people accept
spiritual aid from these beings, they can understand spiritual science. The fact that we can relate positively to spiritual science is
thanks to these cosmic beings who are behind us when we think
anthroposophical thoughts.

But the human race behaves boorishly towards these helpers.
It ignores them. This leads the world into increasingly tragic conditions. More and more spiritual beings move among us whose
language we ought to understand. And we only understand
them when we absorb what emanates from them: the content of
spiritual science.

> You see, it can still seem relatively harmless to people today to think
> the automatic, lifeless thoughts that arise when we grasp the min-
> eral world and the mineral aspect in plants, the mineral in animals,
> the mineral in people. We might say that the modern person delights
> in these thoughts; as materialists they feel comfortable with them
> because only these thoughts are thought today. But just consider
> how it would be if people continued to think in this way, if peo-
> ple really produced nothing other than these kinds of thoughts up
> to the moment in the eighth millennium when the moon existence
> reunites with the earth. What would happen then? Well, the beings I
> have just mentioned will gradually come down to the earth, Vulcan
> beings, Vulcan super-humans, Venus super-humans, Mercury super-
> humans, Sun super-humans and so on will unite with the earth's
> existence. But if humanity continues to meet them only with opposi-
> tion, earth existence in the course of the next millennia will slide into
> chaos. Earthly humanity will indeed be able to carry on developing

its intellect in an automatic way [...] but the fullness of human nature will not be involved in this intellect, and people will have no relation to the beings who want to reach towards them and into earthly existence. And all the beings that are thought in an erroneous way by humanity, the beings thought in an erroneous way because the shadowy intellect only thinks what is mineral, thinks [only] in gross material terms, we could say, in the mineral world, in the plant-, animal-, and even the human kingdom; these human thoughts that have no reality will become reality at a stroke when the moon unites with the earth. And out of the earth will spring up a terrible breed of beings whose character will lie between the mineral and the plant kingdoms as automaton-like beings with a superabundance of reason, with an intense reasoning. This movement will gain ground over the earth which will be covered as though by a net, by a web of terrible spiders, spiders of gigantic wisdom, but whose organization does not reach even to the level of a plant; terrible spiders that will be enmeshed in one another, that will imitate in their external movements what people have thought up with their shadowy intellect which remained impervious to being stimulated by what was supposed to come through a new Imagination, and generally through spiritual science. Everything that people think in thoughts of this nature, which are unreal, will turn into beings. And just as the earth is enveloped by a layer of air, or as it is sometimes covered by a swarm of locusts, so it will be covered by terrible mineral-vegetable spiders that are very intelligent but are enmeshed in each other in a terribly malicious way [aber furchtbar bösartig sich ineinander spinnen]. And human beings, to the extent that they have not enlivened their shadowy intellectual concepts, will be obliged, instead of uniting their being with the beings who have wanted to descend since the last third of the nineteenth century, to unite their being with these terrible mineral-vegetable spider creatures. They will even live together with these spider creatures and will have to find their further progress in cosmic existence in the evolution these spider creatures then follow.[103]

We can look once again at the information given by the spiritual researcher and ask ourselves whether in our present time we can already discern signs of this being realized. Yes: we can see such signs in the phenomenon of computers, in the World Wide Web which is about to pervade our whole life. A glance at children and young people who are addicted to or dependent on continuous consumption of computer games, to killing games for example, tells us that this terrible future has already begun. Parents watch helplessly as their children are sucked into a virtual world which occupies the children entirely and renders them incapable of meeting the requirements of real life like school, training, education in general. Their Ego is hollowed out, their soul dries up, and they can turn into violent thugs or even into murderers.[104]

As one of multiple examples, it was said of Tim K who ran amok on 11 March 2009 at a school at Winnenden {in Germany} and shot dead 15 people, that he had a rigid, unfeeling expression when he entered the building to carry out his intentions. He did this in an ice-cold, automaton-like manner. He had become an egoless shell possessed by a demon.

Thanks to Rudolf Steiner's insights we can prepare for this future. This will involve a technical preparation on the one hand, and a moral one on the other. What is meant by this is that technological devices will increasingly have a being-like and moral quality, and that the cosmic-spiritual beings who accompany humankind will help in this battle. An additional factor is that the spiders mentioned above arise out of the unspiritual thinking of modern humanity. In other words: with our thinking we comprehend and understand the world and the beings that operate in it. Our thoughts are realities and we are responsible for what we think and how we think and for how future humanity will have to live.

The experience of the esotericist becomes more and more clear to us:

Thoughts create reality.

NOTES

1   Rudolf Steiner: *Vorträge und Kurse über christlich-religiöses Wirken V* (Lectures and courses on Christianity) (GA 346), 2ⁿᵈ edition, 2001, p. 185. (English edition: *The Book of Revelation and the Work of the Priest*, 1998.)

2   Rudolf Steiner: *Occult Science* (GA 13).

3   Rudolf Steiner: *Life Between Death and Rebirth* (GA 141).

4   Rudolf Steiner: *Theosophy* (GA 9).

5   See note 4.

6   See note 3.

7   Friedrich Nietzsche: *Gedichte* (Poems), Stuttgart 1978.

Dem unbekannten Gotte
Noch einmal, eh ich weiterziehe
und meine Blicke vorwärts sende,
heb ich vereinsamt meine Hände
zu dir empor, zu dem ich fliehe,
dem ich in tiefster Herzenstiefe
Altäre feierlich geweiht,
daß allezeit
mich deine Stimme wieder riefe.

Darauf erglüht tief eingeschrieben
das Wort: Dem unbekannten Gotte.
Sein bin ich, ob ich in der Frevler Rotte
auch bis zur Stunde bin geblieben:
Sein bin ich—und fühl die Schlingen,
die mich im Kampf darniederziehn
und, mag ich fliehn,
mich doch zu seinem Dienste zwingen.

Ich will dich kennen, Unbekannter,
du tief in meine Seele Greifender,
mein Leben wie ein Sturm Durchschweifender,
du Unfaßbarer, mir Verwandter!
Ich will dich kennen, selbst dir dienen.
Friedrich Nietzsche, 1864

8   Rudolf Steiner: *Geistige Zusammenhänge in der Gestaltung des men-schlichen Organismus* (Spiritual aspects in the formation of the human organism) (GA 218). Dornach, 5th edition 2011, page 107. (English edition: *Spirit as Sculptor of the Human Organism*, 2014.)

9   The Ego can purify its lower sheaths (members-of-being) during many earthly lives. Thus the astral body is transformed into spirit-self, the etheric body into life-spirit, and the physical body into spirit-human. This last should not be imagined in material terms, but such that we can say: the matter of the physical body is completely spiritualized by the purifying work of the Ego and ceases to be matter.

10 Rudolf Steiner: *Geisteswissenschaftliche Menschenkunde* (Spiritual-scientific study of man) (GA 107), Dornach, 6th edition 2011. (English edition: *Disease, Karma and Healing*, 2013.)

11 See note 10, page 328.

12 Rudolf Steiner: *Heilpädagogischer Kurs* (Curative Education) (GA 317). Dornach, 8th edition 1995. (English edition: *Education for Special Needs*, 2014.)

13 See note 12, page 96.

14 Wilhelm zur Linden: *Blick durchs Prisma. Lebensbericht eines Arztes*, Frankfurt a. M., 4th edition 1964, pp. 274-279.

15 Johann Wolfgang v. Goethe: *Faust*, Part I, Faust's study. Verses 1334-1335. Munich 1988.

16 Rudolf Steiner: *Theosophy* (GA 9). Dornach, 33rd edition 2013, p. 50.

17 Rudolf Steiner: *Allgemeine Menschenkunde als Grundlage der Päd-agogik* (Knowledge of man as the basis of teaching) (GA 293). Dornach, 9th edition 1988. (English edition: *Study of Man*, 2004.)

18 See note 17, p. 126.

19 In the teachers' meeting, Rudolf Steiner responded to questions from the teachers. He covered pedagogical and didactic questions, and gave a full picture of certain children who came up for discussion. See: *Konferenzen mit den Lehrern der Freien Waldorschule 1919-1924* (Meetings with teachers at the Free Waldorf School 1919-1924) (GA 300a-c). Volume III: meetings 1923-1924. Meeting on 3 July 1923. Dornach 1975. (English edition: *Faculty Meetings*, 1999.)

20 See note 19, p. 70.

21 Stefan Leber: *Lehrer-Rundbrief* (Newsletter for teachers). Private publication.

[22] Gisbert Husemann, Johannes Tautz (Editor): *Der Lehrerkreis um Rudolf Steiner, Nachruf für Bettina Mellinger*. (The teachers and Rudolf Steiner: obituary for Bettina Mellinger.)

[23] When we read these lectures we can see why Rudolf Steiner wanted to give them to the priests alone. But they have been published, and keeping them secret is no longer possible.

[24] Rudolf Steiner: *Vorträge und Kurse über christlich-religiöses Wirken* (Lectures and courses on religion and Christianity) (GA 346). Dornach, 2nd edition 2001, p. 11. (English edition: *The Book of Revelation and the Work of the Priest*, 1998.)

[25] The New Testatment: Revelation of St John, 9:7-11, in the translation by Jon Madsen, p. 566.

[26] See note 24, p. 184.

[27] See note 24, p. 186.

[28] Rudolf Steiner: *Erziehung und Unterricht aus Menschenerkenntnis* (Education and teaching out of knowledge of the human being) (GA 302a). Dornach, 4th edition 1993. p. 135. (English edition: *Balance in Teaching*, 2007.)

[29] See note 28, p. 137.

[30] See note 28, p. 137.

[31] Rudolf Steiner: *Vorträge und Kurse über christlich-religiöses Wirken* (Lectures and courses on religion and Christianity) (GA 346). Dornach, 2nd edition 2001, p. 235. (English edition: *The Book of Revelation and the Work of the Priest*, 1998.)

[32] See note 31, p. 236.

[33] See note 31, p. 237.

[34] See note 31, p. 238.

[35] We will go into the Sorat impulse in more detail later on. He is the sun demon who opposes the healing up-building forces of Christ.

[36] Rudolf Steiner: *Die Apokalypse des Johannes* (The apocalypse of St John) (GA 104). Dornach, 8th edition, 2006, p. 243. (English edition: *The Apocalypse of St John*, 2004.)

[37] See note 36, p. 227.

[38] Niall Ferguson: *Der falsche Krieg* (The Pity of War). Munich 2001.

[39] Rudolf Steiner: *Zeitgeschichtliche Betrachtungen* (GA 173a-c), Dornach, 2nd edition 2014. (English edition: *The Karma of Untruthfulness*, 2005.)

[40] Rudolf Steiner: *Die soziale Grundforderung unserer Zeit. In geänderter Zeitlage* (GA 186). Dornach, 3rd edition, 1990. (English edition: *The Challenge of the Times*, 1941.)

41 In a lecture given in Berlin, Rudolf Steiner describes the nature of
    David Lloyd George in detail and in a positive light with regard
    to the rejuvenation of humanity, where he presents Lloyd George
    as an examplar of this rejuvenation. See Rudolf Steiner: *Menschli-
    che und menschheitliche Entwicklungswahrheiten* (Truths concerning
    development of the individual and of humanity) (GA 176). Dor-
    nach, 2nd edition. 1982. (English edition: *The Karma of Materialism*,
    1998.) See also the article on this theme by Klaus Dumke in the
    periodical *Anthroposophie*, St John's Tide 2008.
42 See note 40, page 66.
43 Rudolf Steiner: *Zeitgeschichtliche Betrachtungen* (GA 173c). Dornach,
    2nd edition, 2014, p. 136-138. (English edition: *The Karma of Untruth-
    fulness*, 2005.)
44 See note 43, page 139.
45 See note 43, page 140.
46 See note 43, page 142.
47 See note 43, page 143.
48 See the article on Northcliffe and Lloyd George in *Der Große
    Brockhaus*. Volume 15, Leipzig, 18th edition, 1932. 1932 edition.
49 Rudolf Steiner: *Zeitgeschichtliche Betrachtungen* (GA 173a). Lecture
    of 4 December 1926. Dornach, 4th edition, 1910. (English edition: *The
    Karma of Untruthfulness*, 2005.)
50 Rudolf Steiner: *Wahrspruchworte* (Truth-wrought Words) (GA 40).
    Dornach, 9th edition, 2005, page 127.
    Der deutsche Geist hat nicht vollendet,
    Was er im Weltenwerden schaffen soll.
    Er lebt in Zukunftsorgen hoffnungsvoll;
    Er hofft auf Zukunfttaten lebensvoll;
    In seines Wesens Tiefen fühlt er mächtig
    Verborgnes, das noch reifend wirken muß.
    Wie darf in Feindesmacht verständnisloss
    Der Wunsch nach seinem Ende sich beleben,
    Solang da Leben sich ihm offenbart,
    Das ihn in Wesenswurzeln schaffend hält?

51 See also the chapter on 'The human Ego and spiritual economy in
    its development.'
52 Anthony C. Sutton: *Wall Street and the Rise of Hitler*. Clairview
    Books, 2010. 'The remaining four members of the American I.G.
    board were prominent American citizens and members of the

Wall Street financial elite: C.E. Mitchell, chairman of National City Bank and the Federal Reserve Bank of New York; Edsel B. Ford, president of Ford Motor Company; W.C. Teagle, another director of Standard Oil of New Jersey; and, Paul Warburg, first member of the Federal Reserve Bank of New York and chairman of the Bank of Manhattan Company. In brief, in the words of Dr. von Schnitzler: "Thus, in acting as it had done, I.G. contracted a great responsibility and constituted a substantial aid in the chemical domain and decisive help to Hitler's foreign policy, which led to war and to the ruin of Germany. Thus, I must conclude that I.G. is largely responsible for Hitler's policy."'

53   Rudolf Steiner: *Die Kernpunkte der socialen Frage in den Lebensnotwendigkeiten der Gegenwart und Zukunft* (GA 23). Dornach, 6th edition, 1976. (English edition: *Towards Social Renewal*, 1999.)

54   Rudolf Steiner: *Die neue Geistigkeit und das Christus-Erlebnis des zwanzigsten Jahrhunderts* (GA 200). Dornach, 4th edition, 2003. (English edition: *The New Spirituality and the Christ Experience of the Twentieth Century*, 1988.)

55   See note 54, page 38-40.

56   See note 54, page 40.

57   See note 54, page 40.

58   See note 54, page 42.

59   See note 54, page 44.

60   See note 53, page 45.

61   Andrei Bely: *Die silberne Taube* (The Silver Dove). Frankfurt. 1987.

62   Gitta Sereny: *Albert Speer.* Munich 1995, p. 18.

63   See note 62, p. 18. Italicized by the author.

64   Adalbert von Keyserlingk (editor): *Koberwitz 1924.* Stuttgart, 2nd edition 1974, page 37. (English edition: *The Birth of a New Agriculture*, 2009.)

65   Rudolf Steiner: *Menschenwesen, Menschenschicksal und Welt-Entwicklung* (Human being, human destiny and cosmic evolution) (GA 226). Dornach, 5th edition 1988, page 66. (English edition: *Man's Being, His Destiny and World Evolution*, 1966.)

66   Johann Wolfgang v. Goethe: *Dichtung und Wahrheit* (Poetry and Truth), Part One, book 1. In Hamburger edition, Volume 9, Munich 1988, page 44.

67   Rudolf Steiner: *Das Karma des Berufes des Menschen in Anknüpfung an Goethes Leben* (The karma of vocation in connection with the life

of Goethe) (GA 172). Dornach, 6th edition 2002, page 37. (English edition: *The Karma of Vocation*, 2009.)

68 See Hermann Ehret: *Immanuel Hermann Fichte, ein Denker unserer Zeit* (Immanuel Hermann Fichte, a thinker of our time). Stuttgart 1986.

69 See note 68.

70 In: Rudolf Steiner: *Die Rätsel der Philosophie* (GA 18). Dornach, 9th edition 1985, page 181. (English edition: *Riddles of Philosophy*, 2009.)

71 See note 70, page 178.

72 Rudolf Steiner: *Mensch und Welt. Das Wirken des Geistes in der Natur. Über das Wesen der Bienen* (Man and World. The working of the spirit in nature. On the nature of bees) (GA 351). Dornach, 5th edition 1999, page 46. (English edition: *Bees*, 1998.)

73 See note 72, page 46.

74 Ernst Lehrs: *Gelebte Erwartung* (Experienced expectation). Stuttgart 1979.

75 See note 74, page 49.

76 Rudolf Steiner: *Das Leben zwischen dem Tode und der neuen Geburt im Verhältnis zu den kosmischen Tatsachen* (Life between death and rebirth in relation to cosmic facts) (GA 141). Dornach 6th edition 2012, page 62. (English edition: *Between Death and Rebirth*, 1975.)

77 After the burning down of the first Goetheanum, Rudolf Steiner and the houses and facilities on the Goetheanum hill were protected and watched by *guards*, who were mostly young people.

78 Peter Selg (editor): *Anthroposophische Ärtzte* (Anthroposophical doctors). Dornach 2000, page 263.

79 See note 78, page 264.

80 Rudolf Steiner: *Das Prinzip der spirituellen Ökonomie im Zusammenhang mit Wiederverkörperungsfragen: ein Aspekt der geistigen Führung der Menschheit* (The principle of spiritual economy in connection with question of reincarnation: and aspect of the spiritual guidance of humanity) (GA 109). Dornach, 3rd edition, 2000. (English edition: *The Principle of Spiritual Economy*, 1986.)

81 Rudolf Steiner: *Geistige Hierarchien und ihre Widerspiegelung in der physischen Welt* (GA 110). Dornach, 7th edition, 1991, page 172. (English edition: *The Spiritual Hierarchies and the Physical World*, 2008.)

82 Rudolf Steiner: *Die Anthroposophie und ihre Gegner* (Anthroposophy and its opponents) (GA 255b). Dornach. 1st edition, 2003, page 456.

83　　Rudolf Steiner: *Das Prinzip der spirituellen Ökonomie im Zusammenhang mit Wiederverkörperungsfragen* (GA 109). Dornach, 3rd edition, 2000, page 111-113. (English edition: *The Principle of Spiritual Economy*, 1986.)

84　　See note 83, page 57.

85　　See note 83, page 59.

86　　See note 83, page 71.

87　　Karl Werner: *Der heilige Thomas von Aquino* (St Thomas Aquinas). Regensburg 1858, volume I, page 4.

88　　See note 87.

89　　See note 83, page 101.

90　　Rudolf Steiner: *Esoterische Betrachtungen karmischer Zusammenhänge* (Karmic Relationships) (GA 236). Dornach, 6th edition, 1988, page 272. (English edition: *Karmic Relationships, Vol II*, 2015.)

91　　See note 90, page 294.

92　　See note 90, page 296.

93　　See note 90, page 96.

94　　See note 90, page 299.

95　　See note 90, page 300.

96　　See note 90.

97　　*The New Testament: Apocalyptic Sermon on the Mount of Olives*, Matthew 24:35.

98　　Rudolf Steiner: *Das Markus-Evangelium* (GA 139). Dornach, 6th edition. 1985, page 205. (English edition: *The Gospel of St Mark*, 1986.)

99　　Rudolf Steiner: *Geistige Hierarchien und ihre Widerspiegelung in der physischen Welt* (GA 110). Dornach, 7th edition. 1991. (English edition: *The Spiritual Hierarchies and the Physical World*, 2008.)

100　　See note 99, page 172.

101　　In: Rudolf Steiner: *Perspektiven der Menschheitsentwicklung* (Perspectives of human development) (GA 204), Dornach 1979. (English edition: *Materialism and the Task of Anthroposophy*, 1987.)

102　　See note 101, page 242.

103　　See note 101, page 244.

104　　Sergei O. Prokofieff: *Von der Beziehung zu Rudolf Steiner: das Mysterium der Grundsteinlegung* (On the relationship to Rudolf Steiner: the mystery of the laying of the Foundation Stone). Dornach, 2nd edition. 2011, page 133. (English edition: *Relating to Rudolf Steiner*, 2008.)

A note from the publisher

For more than a quarter of a century, **Temple Lodge Publishing** has made available new thought, ideas and research in the field of spiritual science.

Anthroposophy, as founded by Rudolf Steiner (1861-1925), is commonly known today through its practical applications, principally in education (Steiner-Waldorf schools) and agriculture (biodynamic food and wine). But behind this outer activity stands the core discipline of spiritual science, which continues to be developed and updated. True science can never be static and anthroposophy is living knowledge.

Our list features some of the best contemporary spiritual-scientific work available today, as well as introductory titles. So, visit us online at **www.templelodge.com** and join our emailing list for news on new titles.

If you feel like supporting our work, you can do so by buying our books or making a direct donation (we are a non-profit/ charitable organisation).

office@templelodge.com

TEMPLE LODGE
For the finest books of Science and Spirit